The Art of Buying & Selling Real Estate

Featuring Interviews With Top Real Estate Agents in California

Prominence Publishing

The Art of Buying & Selling Real Estate: Featuring Interviews With Top Real Estate Agents in California Copyright © 2015 by Prominence Publishing.

Special thank you to our editor Sally Jo McKean.

For information contact Prominence Publishing:
www.prominencepublishing.com

ISBN: 978-1519691552

First Edition: December 2015

Second Edition: August 2017

Printed in the United States of America

CONTENTS

Important Note 1

Introduction..3

From Commercial to Residential Real Estate

By Danny Alvarez 4

Real Estate as a Second Career

By Annette Marchain... 14

I Chose a Positive Career in a Beautiful Area

By Duarte A. Teixeira 29

How I Help My Clients Buy and Sell in Two Different Counties

By Denise Aquila 44

Developing the Art of Listening

By Mark Hoadley.. 57

34 Years in Real Estate and Still Sane

By Kathy Bartle.. 81

My Journey to a Career in Real Estate

By Rudy LaBrada 97

Real Estate Found Me

By Stacy Young 109

Perseverance Counts

By Cecily Tippery..127

My Real Estate Story

By Roy Tedsen 137

From Beverly Hills/Hollywood to a Career in Real Estate

By Scott Histed 153

Choosing A Real Estate Career

Yashu Toprani 165

Why I Enjoy Making Real Estate As Easy As Possible For My Clients

Quincy Virgilio 175

I Built My Career by Helping Families

By Tony Ayon 188

Conclusion 200

Important Note

We have put a great deal of care into this book, not only in choosing the best contributors on the subject of real estate but also in the presentation of their material. Prominence Publishing, Suzanne Doyle-Ingram and all contributing authors are not responsible for any errors or omissions or for any results that you may have or may not have after applying this information. Your use of the information in this book is at your own risk.

The Use of the Word Realtor®

A Realtor® is a member of the National Association of Realtors®. We understand that the term Realtor® should never be used as a substitute for "real estate agent." Therefore, when we use the term Realtor® in this book, we are not using it lightly, and we do not mean for it to be generically exchanged for "real estate agent."

The Realtors® in this book are actually members of the the National Association of Realtors®.

The title of Realtor® means they are more than just a real estate practitioner. Realtors® adhere to a strict Code of Ethics that protects clients, the public, and other real estate agents.

Although the word REALTOR® is often spelled in full capitol letters, we specifically chose to spell it in lower case letters (eg. Realtor®) throughout the book to make it a more relaxing reading experience for our readers.

Introduction

Thank you for your interest in this book. We have gone to great lengths to source some of the top Real Estate Professionals from California. In fact, it took quite some time to find exactly the right people for this project. We had to weed through a lot of applicants before we decided on these participants. Why? Because we wanted to feature people who are not only true experts at what they do, but who are also ethical, good people. We are proud to let you know that the content you are about to read has even exceeded our own expectations when we first set out to publish this book.

The co-authors of this book were truly a delight to work with! And if you are fortunate enough to be working with one of them, consider yourself lucky too.

When it comes to real estate, homeowners often have more questions than answers and often don't know who to trust for the best advice. They may have a friend or family member who has recently entered the real estate field, and they can feel pressured to list their home with them or look for houses with them. There are so many real estate agents out there, how do you choose? It is our hope that the information in this book will help make your real estate journey a little easier.

This book is for homeowners who are looking to sell their home and get the maximum asking price, as well as for new home buyers who are just starting out in real estate and perhaps looking to buy their first home.

In the chapters that follow, you will gain strategies, tips and highly valuable information from a diverse range of Realtors® from all parts of California. These professionals will provide you with the knowledge that you need so you can make decisions based on advice from their years of experience.

To your success,

Suzanne Doyle-Ingram

Prominence Publishing

From Commercial to Residential Real Estate

By Danny Alvarez

Really loving where you live makes it easy to sell real estate there. I have the best job in the world. I have been in the real estate business for 25 years, with 17 of those years spent in Santa Cruz.

What I love about what I do is that every client and every property is unique, especially in Santa Cruz. It was quite interesting how I ended up in Santa Cruz. In 1998, my then fiancée and I were living in Richmond, Virginia, and we had decided to move back to the West Coast. We weren't exactly sure where we wanted to settle, so we decided to take an entire summer off and just explore. We got in our vehicle with our suitcases, our backpacks, and a mission to find the place where we wanted to start our family together. We drove across the country, and decided we would look in earnest starting somewhere west of the Rockies.

In the middle of the trip, on July 4th weekend, we rolled into Santa Cruz. It was one of those picture perfect days. It was about 70 to 72 degrees, no humidity, and a couple little puffy white clouds in the otherwise clear big blue sky. It was one of those amazing sort of refreshing days. You could wear a long sleeve shirt, and you could wear no shirt, and you were comfortable.

We fell in love with Santa Cruz then and there and never left.

Previously, back in 1990, I was in Los Angeles, and I was in the building trades as a general contractor. I still am a licensed general contractor as I keep my license active. That is an asset for me in real estate because I always look critically for things when I walk into a house. I just see these things naturally because I have been trained to do this for a big part of my life.

Santa Cruz is a little hamlet on the sea. We are separated from Silicon Valley by the Santa Cruz Mountains. There is no real development in those mountains except for sprinkled homes throughout. So, the real population is amassed along the coast, and at the north end of Santa Cruz all the way up to Half Moon Bay. It is probably one of the smallest per square mile populations in the country. There is nothing there, it is virgin. It is a beautiful scenic coastline. Generally, there is no traffic piling down from the north. To the south end of the county, you have lots of villas. That is a big farming community. It is the capital of strawberries and artichokes with a huge percentage of the total national gross strawberry and artichoke production coming from there.

My Real Estate Roots

When I left Los Angeles and moved back to the East Coast, I sold my home in Los Angeles. I sold it myself. I was not planning on doing a "for sale by owner", but I thought, "I wonder what my house is worth," because I knew I was going to be moving back East. I went around the neighborhood and I researched the different marketing tactics the agents were doing. I grabbed all the flyers. I came home and spread them out on the table. I was looking at prices and numbers and the different ways they were marketing. Then I said, "I think I can do this."

I created a flyer and took out an ad. I sold my home in the first open house I had - mind you, it was a very hot market in 1990 – and I ended up using an agent who represented the buyer and of course I paid that agent a commission. The result for me was that I had so much fun doing it that when I got to Richmond, instead of just getting right back into the construction business, I decided I would try real estate. I took my license and did the exam. In those days, we had to wait 30 days for the results.

While I was waiting, I played golf. On Labor Day, I happened to be paired up with three other gentlemen who were off that day. By the fifth hole, I did not realize I had been interviewed for a job. In golf, if you do not know who the stranger is you are paired up with, it is an easy way to find out information like, "So what do you do and where are you from." My new golf friend had found out I just moved from California, I was a licensed contractor, and I had taken the real estate test and was waiting for the result. It turned out he was a commercial broker, and he liked who I was and how I carried myself. By the fifth hole, he asked me to meet him at his office and at the end of that meeting, he hired me.

So my first eight years in real estate was as a commercial broker and that is quite a different animal. I was really glad to have that as my basis because it is akin to getting a pass in the bar exam in real estate, if you will. The contracts and the numbers are a huge part of the business in commercial, versus the heart and the home of residential real estate. It is a much simpler equation to solve in a house. It is an emotional attraction for a nest most of the time. In commercial, it is a whole other ball of wax.

During those eight years, I rose quickly. Within a couple of years, I started getting approached by the larger brokerage firms. Eventually I did join one of the top three largest firms in Richmond, Virginia at that time, Robinsons Sigma. They put me in charge of the head of the Retail Division. In 1996, I was the number one agent in that company and had the largest grossing deal that year which was a $6.5 million sale. I was the top producing agent in the company that year. They are now a CB Ellis firm in Richmond.

I moved to Santa Cruz in 1998 and focused on both commercial and residential real estate. Some years, I will do 20 percent commercial. Last year, I did about 40 percent commercial. Then other years, I will have only one commercial deal. Mostly I focus on residential sales, buyers and sellers. I am a great buyer's agent in that I am a people person. I can quickly understand what people really want and are looking for. I do not think that can be said of a vast majority of agents who do not really listen and appreciate what the people are really looking for or wanting. I hear that a lot from people who are frustrated with the agents they are working with; they are not listening, they keep showing stuff they do not really want. I have a knack for working with buyers and sellers. I was the number one buyer's agent in my company last year. I sell everything from medium priced homes to luxury homes. I am working on a $5 million sale right now - an offer for a beach front property.

I am with David Lyng & Associates. When I moved here, I bought a house through an agent who was just getting started at The Real Estate Center. That was in 1997. By 2004, I had purchased The Real Estate Center from the broker and ran it until 2008, when I was approached by David Lyng. He purchased my company and the building I owned downtown and I went to work for him. I got a good package deal. It was an offer I could not refuse.

Our company is known for luxury real estate. We have been number one, with an average list price over a million dollars, for approximately the last 15 years in a row. We have offices in Carmel, Watsonville, Capitola - our main office, and one here in Santa Cruz which is my former building.

Many of my clients come by referral. I listen to them, they feel taken care of, and they say to their friends, "Hey, you guys should use Danny." Commercial deals just kind of come to me. Sometimes, I see it, and I think, "I have gotten to know some of my residential clients that are well-to-do. Do they like to invest their money?" Many of them love commercial real estate. In fact, I just had lunch with an old client I have not seen in a while. We reconnected and he has some money to spend - up to $3 to $4 million – and asked that I keep my eyes open. I already have something in mind to talk to him about.

Community Work

I was on the board of Kids on Broadway, a non-profit theater group for children aged 7 to 16. They do Broadway plays and production plays. It is very homespun, homegrown, and wonderful. My daughter was in it and I was on the board for a couple of years.

I have different projects I like to donate to, such as a homeless shelter. I have also been a coach for both soccer and volleyball at the school my three daughters attend and I support the booster club for the athletic department at Santa Cruz High. I have also donated to the golf team at the high school.

Buying a Home in Santa Cruz

When buying a home in Santa Cruz, you need to know who you are up against in a competitive market. Right now, we are in a very hot market. Having a savvy agent who is well networked is very important. Right now, we have just over one thousand agents in our local area. Ten percent of those thousand agents are doing 90 percent of the business of listings and sales.

In helping my buyer, they need to be pre-approved with everything prepared and ready to go. I need to know how much money we can show in an offer that they can put down. I need to know their financials inside out so I know how to utilize their strengths or their weaknesses.

Once we are in the house, I make sure we have the right inspections done on the house to make sure they are not buying a house with problems. I do all the due diligence on that.

On the flipside, when representing the seller, I encourage them to do as many of the inspections that they can tolerate. At the very least, they need a pest report, which is the biggest bang for your dollar. You can get a pest inspection for under $200, and if the results indicate you have a pest problem, that will be about 90 percent of the major cost in repairs that are required in a house. On that one inspection report, you will get information about: dry rot, termite, beetles, pests... all of those things. Those are usually the most expensive items that come up.

The reason that pre-inspections are so important is because the buyer is going to do their own inspections and find out anyway. If repairs are under $1,000, that's reasonable and often they will accept that and take it as is. But if the repairs are going to be $3,000, $5,000, $12,000, and the seller does not want to negotiate, then the deal falls apart and the house is back on the market. The difference is that now we have a report that was performed by their inspector, and we have to disclose the report to the next buyer. It is much better to do a pre-inspection so all the cards are on the table from the beginning.

With a listing, time is money. You do not want to be sitting out on the market for more than you need to because it brings questions about what is wrong with the house. One way to nip that in the bud is to get at least a pest inspection; secondly, the home inspection, thirdly, the chimney inspection, fourthly, the septic inspection—we have lots of septic out here— and, finally, a well inspection. All of these are key items and if anything is wrong with them, it could be major. All those inspections together, if you did them all, might run you $1,500.

Disclosure is important. In this county, an agent who represents a buyer and does not disclose known information about a well, is wide open for a lawsuit.

When I have a listing, I survey the home myself and prioritize a list of repairs that are needed. For example, the hardwood floors might need to be refinished. Perhaps the countertops are dated, it needs paint inside and out, and better landscaping. I get bids from two or three subcontractors so the homeowners can see the projected costs, and I then I operate as a contractor with these subcontractors (Not for profit.) I know how to speak their language, get these bids, and negotiate the prices for my clients. I set all of that up. We do not always go with the cheapest price because you get what you pay for.

After any repairs are completed, then we have the house properly staged - whether it is vacant or occupied. We need to take things in and out and move them around, get rid of that and hide this, so when people walk in, they "Ooh and aah" and not, "Ugh. What?"

David Lyng & Associates were the first to come out with a live video of the property, and we started doing that in 2008. We have a professional videographer that comes to all of our listings, shoots a video of the property; it is really nice when you can see a real crackling fire in the fireplace, bubbles are really bubbling in the hot tub, and when you look out over to the ocean, the waves are really crashing.

It's Not A Deal Until Escrow Closes

I once had a listing with a very tight deadline. The listing was only going to be for six weeks, but I was up for the challenge. The deadline was September 14th because that was the last week left before school started at the university. The homeowner had taken the summer to fix it all up. He finished the floors, painted it, and did all these things to get ready for the market. Then he tried to sell it himself for a month, and it did not work. I got it August 1, but I had it only for six weeks. Three days before my deadline, the homeowner had an open house to show it to renters, and he got six groups of renters who wanted to pay him top dollar. On September 14th, the very last day of our agreement, I got an offer. It was not a full price offer, and they did not want to negotiate. I called my client but I could not reach him. His father called me back to say he was out of the country. Because I couldn't reach him I had to pull it off MLS, per our agreement.

They had decided on their tenant and they were going to move forward with that. I had not had any previous dealings with the father, so it was very difficult for me to get anywhere. I was at a dead end.

The buyer who had made the offer wanted it as an investment. It was a great offer but my client's father was dead set on not wanting to respond.

Two weeks later, I knew the son was back and although he was a cut-and-dry type of person, much like his father, I felt that I had some rapport with him. I sent an email and I said, "I do not quite understand why you did not even want to consider countering since these people wanted to buy this as an investment and potentially still would take it even with the tenant you selected. So there is no risk. Imagine one year from now, if you go to try to sell this now, it won't look new and fresh like it does now. And it is going to be beaten by these tenants. I just do not understand. Can you help me out and explain the logic to me." He calls me immediately and he says, "What? They'll buy it? They'll take it with the tenant in now?" I said, "Yes." And within two days, we were in contract, and there was an "All Cash" offer. They closed in three weeks. It pays to be persistent.

Marketing

I hold open houses whenever my clients allow. I think they are very useful and a great way to get your house seen. One of the key things we do to market a home is take beautiful photographs on every property. I put those on an eflyer, and that eflyer is sent to every real estate agent in the county, which is about a thousand real estate agents. It also is sent to the top 100 agents over the hill in Silicon Valley. When they open the email there is a picture, with the prompt to view the video. They click that and the video begins. It is usually just a two-minute video. We find this is way better than some glowy, sugary, overwrought description that many Realtors® use. Pictures work way better than words.

That is how we start off with a bang and get the marketing on the right track.

To get the maximum amount when selling, timing is everything. If given the opportunity, list in the spring. Our spring starts in February in this county, other counties it starts in April and May. February, March are the best months to sell here.

The Process That I Use From Start to Finish

- We meet and preview the home.
- After previewing the home, I put together a CMA, Comparative Market Analysis. I do not do this before I meet because I want to see the house first. In fact, I like doing the CMA with the client at their kitchen table, sitting down, and say, "Let's just go ahead and do it so you could see the process I use and you can ask questions, and then you can help me kick out the costs we all think are mismatched."
- After we do that, I like to go ahead and get our listing agreement solidified because after that, it is time to go to work.
- Then we announce a "Coming Soon" to the company at our office meeting every Wednesday.
- The next thing would be to get the inspections booked, and determine what work needs to be done, depending on their budget.
- We then implement the work, which means me helping them get all the bids, making decisions, and setting up the work schedules.
- At the end of all that, we may change the price on the listing agreement, depending on the scope of work that has been done.
- We also fill out the seller disclosures and sign them so we have them all ready.
- I will also schedule the video shoot and the photography.

- Once we have that done, we put together our eflyer with the video and the photos and announce the open houses.
- Then we post it on MLS and on social media, which is everything from Facebook, Craigslist, LinkedIn, LoopNet, if it is that kind of property, and then all of the other sites, Realtor .com, Zillow, and all of those. My social media person does all that for me.
- Then, I do the Broker's Open on that first Thursday. That eflyer goes out on a Monday or Tuesday. We have a Broker's Open on that Thursday. Then we have two open houses back to back Saturday and Sunday that first weekend.
- The next thing we do is we negotiate an offer.
- Once that offer is accepted, we navigate through escrow and we close.
- And we never forget to celebrate! I like to take most of my clients out in some way or give them a gift certificate to go out for a nice dinner on their own.

I am so glad I made the move out here to Santa Cruz back in 1998. For me, real estate is the easiest and most rewarding job in the world. They say that when you love what you do, you will never work a day in your life. And that is certainly true for me.

About the Author

Danny Alvarez

David Lyng Real Estate
120 Water St
Santa Cruz, CA 95060

Email:danny@santacruzforsale
Website: santacruzforsale.com
Tel: 831-818-4181

Danny Alvarez has been a full time licensed agent/broker since 1990. He has also been a licensed California General Contractor since 1984. From 1990 to 1997 he worked exclusively as a Commercial Broker, winning a Top Producer award in 1996. Danny moved to Santa Cruz with his family in 1997 and has been involved in all aspects of Real Estate, predominantly residential, since then.

In 2004 he took over ownership of the Real Estate Center in Downtown Santa Cruz, which he eventually sold to David & Sally Lyng in 1998 and then joined David Lyng Real Estate as an Associate Broker.

Danny loves what he does and he is energetic, positive and proactive. He has a lot to offer anyone thinking about buying or selling any type of Real Estate.

Real Estate as a Second Career

By Annette Marchain

When I was a young married woman and had my first baby, I was working full-time. After my maternity leave, I very reluctantly went back to work, missing my little daughter terribly. While working, I began the thought that I would like to have a career that allowed me to set my own schedule. With this in mind, I obtained my real estate license, interviewed with a broker, and began working part-time as a real estate agent. Naively, I thought I could do this on the side, but in reality, I ended up working two full-time jobs! I really enjoyed real estate, and had some good clients that I helped, but it became difficult to do both careers due to a huge responsibility that I was given in my telecommunications field.

At the time, I was working for Pacific Telephone in the Federal Government division. We supported the White House, Secret Service, and Department of State. Whenever anyone who had those protections; the President of the United States, members of the First Family, the Vice President, Foreign Dignitaries, and declared candidates for President or Vice President, visited the Los Angeles extended area, we provided all of their communications This was way before wireless. Every service had to be wired in, and we also drove a vehicle equipped with a six line (channel) mobile phone in the motorcades. I was originally on the team tasked with this responsibility, and then I became the single point of contact and liaison for the White House Communications Agency, Secret Service, and Department of State. It was a huge responsibility, requiring me to stay in our command center in the selected hotel, and to be accessible 24-7. With that responsibility, I made the decision to make my real estate license inactive, because if I couldn't do an outstanding job at 100% with a real estate client, I was not going to do it.

I continued my career in telecommunications and information technology as a Senior Account Manager, and enjoyed many experiences, offering "cutting edge" services and solutions to customers such as IBM, Walt Disney Company, Warner Bros., and Sony Entertainment. In the late 1990's, I was offered a very generous early retirement package and I just could not ignore the offer. I left the business and thought that since I had always had my nose in real estate with buying and selling properties, I would go back and get my license again. When I was given my license number, I was pleased to see that it was my original license number!

Things have changed drastically from the mid 1970's to when I came back to real estate in the late 1990's early 2000's. For example, in the 1970's, we were changing from a one page contract to a two page contract, which was huge then, and laughable now! We also had to write in on the contract many of the things that are now boilerplate. We had books containing all the listings, and we picked these up on a weekly basis in order to see what was on the market. Basically, everything was paper based, and back then, the fax was a really new innovation.

When I came back to the business in 2000, the basic residential listing agreement was now a ten page contract and the focus was disclosure, disclosure, disclosure. In California sellers must disclose anything they know about the property, unlike what it was is in the mid '70s when the environment was "let the buyer beware". Now disclosure weighs even more heavily, resulting in an offer today being approximately 24 pages long.

Of course now everything is online. We Realtors® used to be "keepers of all things" in the way of multiple listings. However, now everyone can go online and find homes on their own, and contact a Realtor® when they want to see the property. If buyers are savvy though, they will contact a good Realtor® to help them through the negotiation and the transaction.

South Pasadena, Pasadena, and beyond!

The San Gabriel Valley is my area of expertise because I know all the cities, communities and neighborhoods well. It is a huge area, comprised of about 20 cities. In that valley, the city I focus on the most is my home town, which is South Pasadena, California. South Pasadena is a city, separate from Pasadena. It is not the southern part of Pasadena. This can be confusing for people and Realtors® who are not familiar with the area. We often see out-of-area agents listing homes inappropriately as being located in South Pasadena, when the property is actually in Pasadena. This is one of many reasons that it is not a good idea to have a Realtor® represent you on a sale or purchase who is out of the area and not familiar with neighborhoods, etc.

South Pasadena is a lovely small town. It has excellent schools, and is both freeway and surface street close to downtown Los Angeles. With minimal traffic on the 110 freeway, it takes about twenty minutes, with traffic it could be forty-five minutes to an hour. However, we now have the Metro Gold Line train that is fabulous - it goes right through South Pasadena, with a platform stop in the sweet Mission District of South Pasadena. You hop on the train and you are at Union Station in LA in no time, and you do not have to worry about the traffic. From Union Station, you can connect to many other metro lines, or Amtrak and get just about anywhere.

Now let's talk about Pasadena. A much larger city than South Pasadena, and widely known for the Rose Parade and Rose Bowl, Pasadena is a metropolitan city with many distinct neighborhoods. Architecture from many eras abounds here, with grand examples of Greene and Greene Craftsman design, the lovely Gamble House being the crown jewel; Victorian, Spanish Colonial, Italian Renaissance, and many others. Home pricing in Pasadena spans from $400,000 condos to $24,000,000 estates. You have it all here! Shops, entertainment, museums, and an array of restaurants make Pasadena a wonderful place to live, work and visit. We have museums such as the Norton Simon Museum, and the Huntington Gardens which actually sit right in San Marino, which is adjacent to Pasadena. A couple of times a year throughout Pasadena, we have Art Night where you can tour various sites and see performances and exhibitions. And again, the Metro Gold Line goes right through the city with many stops along the way.

Old Town Pasadena is just wonderful, and has become quite the destination. This area was transformed from a somewhat seedy area at Colorado and Fair Oaks in the 1960s, to a destination spot in the late 1970's, utilizing the original beautiful buildings and bringing in unique shops and places to eat. I feel a special connection with Old Pasadena, because my grandparents moved to Pasadena from New York in the early 1900's. Working for Procter and Gamble as a Facilities Manager, my grandfather, William Raab, was sent out to Pasadena to open one of Proctor and Gamble's facilities, and ended up staying here. He loved to cook, and so when he retired, he and a friend owned and operated five little restaurants here in the city. My roots are definitely in Pasadena.

Most of my transactions are in Pasadena and South Pasadena, but I definitely cover the surrounding cities and communities. San Gabriel Valley is a rich fabric of cities and neighborhoods and I know them well!

When I was dating my husband and planning to get married, we were looking for a place to live. Once I introduced him to the foothills here in the Sierra Madre area, he was smitten. I could not get him to move to South Pasadena where I originally wanted to live. However, he won out, and I am happy here in this special place, where we have a lovely neighborhood with great neighbors, wildlife and a great view of the local mountain range. We've been here for 30 years! Sierra Madre is half the size of South Pasadena, and it is known as the Foothill Village. It is a little town that has a population of about ten thousand people. There are tons of trails where you can go into Angeles National Forest. It is just a lovely little place. One of the famous things that Sierra Madre is known for is the Wisteria Festival. In the Guinness Book of World Records as the largest blossoming vine, the Wisteria plant known as the Purple Lady, is huge and absolutely fragrant with beautiful purple blooms. Each year, around May, the city holds a tour of the home where the plant resides, and has a festival in its downtown area, with art, craft, and food kiosks. It is quite the day!

We have the typical small town 4th of July parade where practically everyone is in the parade. South Pasadena does the same thing. The two cities have a synergy, between the two of them. Sierra Madre is about half the size of South Pasadena geographically and population wise, but they share a very similar feeling. Also, the movie "The Invasion of the Body Snatchers," was filmed here in Sierra Madre in 1952.

Consultative Selling

My specialty is consultative selling. I believe in sitting down with the client and finding out what they really want to achieve, and looking at all aspects of that goal. This is really important because they need to share and be open with me. If I do not know their financial position or what they are really trying to accomplish – if they're holding their cards to their chest - it just does not work. Eventually, something comes out that can just sideswipe the entire process. I cannot help them unless I know what they are trying to accomplish. My clients want to work with a seasoned professional, and spend the time to tell me what they want to accomplish.

This approach has worked well for me with all of my careers and definitely in real estate. I think this is a little bit different, since I am not looking for a quick sale in order to make a quick commission. Unfortunately, some other Realtors® look at that end result for themselves, and do not always think about the client's needs as much as they should.

In my business, I have noticed a trend over the past few years. I often represent Baby Boomers who are selling their homes to move closer to their children or grandchildren. They are not necessarily downsizing, although in some instances that is the case. For instance, I have clients now who are moving from Pasadena to the Manhattan Beach area to be closer to their children and only grandchildren. They are not going to necessarily retire; they will be doing many things, and still working, but want some flexibility. Due to the cost of real estate in the beach cities of Southern California, they will be downsizing their house, but paying about the same or more than what they will be obtaining from selling their lovely home here.

I have a wonderful couple who has done just the opposite; selling their large property overlooking the Pacific Ocean in Palos Verdes, and have purchased a luxury condominium in Pasadena. No more landscape upkeep! Now they're treated like royalty in their new "digs". They desire it! There are many examples of this type of move and transition with clients whom I have been blessed to work with over the years.

Referrals

Approximately 90% of my business comes from referrals from past clients, friends, family, and from organizations where I'm a member. When past clients refer someone to me, especially one of their family members, it is the highest of compliments. I am truly blessed to have wonderful past clients, who is most cases have become close friends, almost like family! Another referral source for me is Business Network International, or BNI. I am in a local chapter, Referral Resources here in Pasadena, and I am a founding member. This group of business professionals has been a great resource of referrals for me, and I have actually helped several members sell their own homes. Referrals also come from friends and family.

Community Involvement

I am a member of the Women's Council of Realtors®, the twelfth largest professional women's organization in the nation. It incorporates directly into the National Association of Realtors®. I am a 2015 District Vice President, Women's Council of Realtors®, State of California. This is an elected position, voted on by the State Governing Board, and I was just voted in again for 2016 as a District Vice President. I am responsible for mentoring and assisting local Women's Council of Realtors® Networks in District 4. In the past, I have been a President for several years, of our local San Gabriel Valley Network.

One of the organizations that I am also passionate about is the Friends of the Rialto. I am on the Board of Directors of this group that is dedicated to saving and restoring a lovely old theater in South Pasadena. It was the one and only movie theater in South Pasadena for decades, and also used for dance rehearsals, etc.

Being involved in community issues and groups is very important to me, and I give generously of my time, as well as portions of my commissions, to charities.

Berkshire Hathaway HomeServices, California Properties is my brokerage, and I am proud to be in the top 7% of the Berkshire Hathaway HomeServices Realtors® in the nation.

Selling a Home

The most important advice I can give to anyone who will be selling their home is to engage and listen to an experienced Realtor®. Of course, I would hope that I am that Realtor®!

There are three important pieces to having your home sell ion the market, sort of like a three legged stool. If one isn't represented correctly, the stool will not stand.

Pricing: Your property is priced right for the market. Is the market a seller market, a buyer market, or an even market? What are comparable properties selling for in your area? This is where an experienced Realtor® makes all the difference in the world. Do not think that you can look your home up on Zillow and get accurate information. It is actually most often 8-10% off.

Condition: Next is curb and interior appeal. Keep up good appearances - most buyers want to go in and see that they can just move in. Make the home as clean as possible inside, depersonalize things as much as possible, and sometimes staging works really well. I recommend staging especially if it is going to be a vacant house. Buyers need to envision how furniture and furnishings can be arranged in the space. It has been proven that homes often sell more quickly when staged.

Marketing: Your property needs to have as much exposure to potential buyers as possible. I do this by making sure that there are nice looking brochures, normally a floor plan, and print advertizing. Even though there is a thought that everyone looking for homes will be looking on-line, you never know where your buyer may come from, so you need to do it all. A buyer could initially see an ad in the newspaper or a magazine, and then look it up on-line. With that, I also always host a Broker Open House, as well as several public Open

Houses. Finally, I send out announcements about the property, and share it with my office and all my contacts and former clients as well as BNI.

I hold Open Houses for my own listings. I always hold a Broker Open House (with food!) and then I have at least one public Open House. I strongly believe in exposure, exposure, exposure, so you need to do Open Houses. Also, if it is a large house, I have someone help me with the Open House.

I view marketing the property as if "presented" to the market. I do more than just input the listing into the Multiple Listing Service (MLS) website. I make sure all the photos are taken, the descriptions are ready to go, the brochures are ready, and the ads are preset. When these are all done, the property is ready to be presented to the market. I then schedule the Broker Open House, which gives Realtors® time to pre-view the property for their clients. I also share the listing ahead of time at our office meeting. We have two Realtor® Associations in this area, and have at least two Broker events every week. At these Broker Opens, I always have something for the agents to eat-- because if you feed them they will come! This is followed by public Open House dates over the weekends. It is critical to make sure you have all those things ready to go, and that they are very professional. I have someone who takes wonderful photos of homes – he is the only one I use because he is very good. People love photos and photos sell. I want to make sure there is an array of good photos of the home on-line, and that I can arrange them as a tour through the property.

Most often, I also have a website created for each listing, using the address of the property as the website address. This gives people the opportunity to take a video tour of the home as well as giving them property information.

Buying a Home

When considering buying a home, and are planning to do this with a loan, the very first thing you need is a pre-approval from a lender. It is critical that you have spoken with a good mortgage professional to see what you would qualify to buy, and then be able to provide a seller with this pre-approval letter as well as proof that you have funds to close and for a down payment. Getting your financing in order is more important now than ever before, because if you find something you really like and want to buy, in order for your offer to be considered by the seller, you need to provide them with a preapproval/prequalification letter from a lender or mortgage professional.

The next most important thing is to work with a full-time experienced Realtor® who knows the area very well. You need to communicate well with them and vice versa and then stick with them. Do not go shopping around with different people. Do not get into the trap of thinking, I need to work with the listing agent, they are going to give me a deal. They are representing the seller, they are not representing you. You need to have your own representation. I cannot stress that enough. Particularly in California, where we are a heavy disclosure state, you need to have your own representation.

Never Stop

I had some dear people I was working with who were selling their sweet home in Pasadena and moving to a home closer to where she actually worked in the Upland area. The Upland area is quite far from Pasadena which is why this commute was one of their issues. Once I listed their home, we had multiple offers, one of which was a really nice VA loan offer. Now, VA loans are a little bit different, but my clients really liked the fact that this was a woman veteran coming back from Iraq. She was a JAG attorney in the military, and was now working for a large attorney firm in Los Angeles. My clients received many offers but they selected this buyer. We moved forward and found their replacement home in Upland. It was the perfect place for them. This was going to be a coordinated closing and we had a closing date that was going to be great. Everything was going to work out nicely. There were only a few days in between each closing, which was great for them because they were going to stay in a hotel for one night.

Then, we had a few little hiccups on the VA loan side. One of the big hiccups was that the buyer decided to take a new job with the L.A. District Attorney's office. She took this new job, right in the middle of the process which is a pretty big "no no" during a VA loan process. This disrupted the entire loan process. She had to go back and redo everything, which was going to cause a huge delay. Now, my poor clients were between a rock and a hard place. Fortunately, I was working with a seasoned professional Realtor® on the other side of the Upland transaction. She and I met for coffee and talked about how we could get this done. This was a trust sale and she actually was a distant relation to the woman who had passed away and to the woman's children who were selling the property. She was able to ask them if they would allow my clients to move in and pay reduced rent for a period of time during the delay.

We were able to work the entire situation out, so that my lovely clients could move into the Upland house. We ended up closing on the Pasadena house while they were already in the Upland house. Sometimes, I think things are meant to happen and you need to make sure it gets done. At one point, we were thinking the entire transaction would just fall apart. It was helpful to know we had backup offers on the Pasadena house. While negotiating, I did advise the buyer's Realtor® that we had backup offers, and if she was not going to get this VA loan done, and it was going to effect my clients any more, then we would cancel the escrow and select one of the backup offers. Unfortunately, sometimes you have to play hard ball. My clients are the most important thing to me. If you are one of my clients, you are golden to me.

Adventures in Real Estate: "Listen to Your Voicemail"

Once I was showing a townhouse to a client. It was a case where you just call the homeowner and leave the message letting her know you are going to be there. So, I did that. I called and I left a message the day before. I also called that morning and said, "We're going to be coming over at ten o'clock." The townhouse had a lockbox so I knew I could get in if she was not home. I took my clients to the townhouse, I retrieved the key, and I knocked on the door. I always knock first. There was no response to my knocking except for the barking of a little dog. It was just a little bark, so I figured it would be fine. I opened the door and walked in announcing myself with a loud, "Hello!" The little dog approached me, a little tiny sweetie, and I went in with my client. This was a three story townhouse. Just as we walked in the door, I heard a sound like water running. Oh my gosh. I asked my clients to wait, as I went up to see if someone left the water on or something. I walked up the stairs very carefully and suddenly I thought, "Oh my goodness, it sounds like someone is in the shower." I peeked into the bedroom and I saw multiple photos of a woman. She was an L.A.P.D. Officer. There were pictures of her with the Chief of Police and I thought, "Oh great, she is in the shower. We are going to interrupt an L.A.P.D. officer when she is in the shower as I am showing this house!" So I carefully backed out and I told my client that maybe someone did not get the message that we were going show it this morning. I said we probably should leave and come back later.

I backed out of the house and locked it all up. As I was walking by her phone, I saw the blinking light on her answering machine, indicating that she had several messages. Perhaps she had never even listened to my messages, but the last thing I wanted to do is surprise an L.A.P.D. Officer as she is coming out of the shower. It was a little surprising because when I entered the townhouse, I was not only talking, I was saying, "Hello, it's Annette Marchain, Realtor®!" I am not quiet. Her dog was barking, too. Luckily she never knew because I never called back to say "Hi, I was there when you were in the shower." That sure was a memorable showing. I did follow up to make anther appointment, and did talk with her live.

Maintaining and Increasing the Value of Your Home

Of all of the home improvement projects out there, one of the cheapest and most beneficial is paint. Freshening your exterior and interior with new paint is really a great thing, and makes it stand out and be more attractive to buyers. If you are wondering what kind of return you are going to get for the projects you decide to complete, you should contemplate what you have in the way of finances to do the projects, and also what tolerance you have to live through the disruption that is innate in some projects. Do you need to do a major upgrade, like tearing out a wall or completely remodeling a kitchen, or do you just need a few small things done?

It's also important to freshen up the exterior. Improve the curb appeal by trimming the landscaping and planting some flowers, etc. These things will help increase the value of the home without spending thousands of dollars. With the drought conditions we currently have here in California, you probably should consider planting some drought tolerant plants and landscaping. A drip watering system is also a good investment here.

Repairs should be done before the property goes on the market. It is not a good thing to be mid remodel when showing the house. Once it is presented to the market, it needs to be ready to roll. I always walk through the home in the beginning, because I can give my clients suggestions about things they can do to increase the value of the home. For example, I have a client who has a big mid-century modern home which has the sprayed "popcorn ceiling." That was really in vogue at the time it was built in the 1970s, but most people hate it now, or have been programmed to hate it. In any case, it was a big question about whether it should be removed. The issues were: it is a messy job, it takes a long time to do, and, will he get a good return on his investment? The answer was, probably not. I suggested he just leave it and let someone else decide if they are going to make those changes.

Realtor® or For Sale By Owner

One of the most important reasons to use a Realtor® when selling your home in California is the fact that we are a disclosure state when it comes to real estate. Failure to disclosure equals liabilities. Homeowners probably do not know about these disclosures and liabilities, and they can really stub their toe or worse because of it. I always use this example; if you needed to have a mole removed on your back, you would not do this yourself. Rather, you would go to a physician to have the mole removed. You want to use a seasoned professional to help you through the process. The same with selling your home. Why wouldn't you use a Realtor®? My services will actually bring you more return in a higher sales price.

It is worth what you pay for that professional. You will get more for your home and you will keep yourself from being in court later.

Negotiation is my specialty, and I will keep you at arm's length from actual face to face negotiation during the transaction. You have an agent working in your best interest. Listing your home with a Realtor® offers much more exposure and statistics say that 97% of homes are sold by another Realtor®.

Buyers should expect good communication from their Realtor® throughout the buying or selling process. Also, they should expect a professional manner in dealing with everything in the process. My clients' best interest is my priority. Buyers should expect a seasoned professional whose foremost goal is to help you meet your goals in a fiduciary manner. As a Realtor®, I am available by phone, text, and email. Quite frankly, I am always available - during the business day, in the evenings, and on weekends. I work many hours during the week.

The Process

When I take a new listing, I inform my clients about all of the disclosures and forms that need to be completed. I go over those on a high level, but then I come back and have a separate meeting with them to go through all of that paperwork in order to make sure that my clients know what they are signing.

Depending on when it is going on the market, I will have photos taken, and discuss with the client what they need to do in the house to get it ready. Then we go through the marketing and showing instructions. The showing instructions are very important, because it needs to be tailored to what is convenient for them and still be able to have the property shown. For example: will it be "appointment only"? Will my office make the appointment by calling the seller? Will I make the appointment? Is there a lockbox for direct access? Do my clients have pets that we need to be concerned about? And so on. I do whatever works for that particular client, and the showing instructions should be personalized and appropriate. If I get the feeling that there is a lot of interest in the property, I announce that we are going to be reviewing offers on a particular day and time. That way, other Realtors® have time to show the property to potential buyers, and then present an offer. It creates a sense of urgency which is kind of a two-way street. It also gives enough time for people to see the property. I give it at least a week to be marketed completely so those who can only get out on weekends have an opportunity to see the property as well.

I believe the key to my success is that I treat all my clients the same as I would a CEO of a large company. They are the owners of their property, their needs must be met and it all must be done on a professional level. My clients deserve to be respected and well taken care of. Nothing satisfies me more than seeing the smiles that come with a successful real estate transaction.

About the Author

Annette Marchain

Berkshire Hathaway HomeServices
– California Properties

626-674-5486 Cell
www.Annette4RealEstate.com
email: AnnetteMarchain@aol.com

Originally licensed in the mid 1970s, Annette took a sabbatical from Real Estate when she was offered an opportunity in the telecommunications industry as the local liaison for the White House and Secret Service. After that assignment, Annette ultimately became the Senior Account Manager responsible for sales to clients such as IBM, Walt Disney Co., Time-Warner and Sony Entertainment.

After many years as a seasoned telecommunications sales professional, Annette made the decision to return to Real Estate, and has pursued her successful career since then with Berkshire Hathaway HomeServices – California Properties. The negotiation skills and professionalism she brought with her are very appreciated by her clients. She is involved in every aspect of the buying and selling transaction in order to ensure a smooth and successful close of escrow for her clients.

Her experience, coupled with her technical and financial knowledge, enable her to market properties with maximum exposure, so that you will sell your property quickly, and save time and money. And when it comes to the transaction, Annette and her team will be there to assist you in dealing with the multiple details and voluminous paperwork involved in today's transactions.

Annette specializes in listing and selling homes in Pasadena, South Pasadena, San Marino, Arcadia, Monrovia, Sierra Madre, and adjoining communities. She certainly knows the area, having been born in Pasadena and raised in South Pasadena. Annette and her husband have resided in Sierra Madre for the past 30 years, and she also owns property in her hometown of South Pasadena. Annette strongly believes in giving back to the community and charities, and generously gives of her time and finances.

Leadership Roles:

- 2009-2010 President Women's Council of Realtors®, San Gabriel Valley Chapter
- 2011 Chairman, Budget and Finance Committee, 2012 Audit Committee, California State Chapter, Women's Council of Realtors®
- 2015 and 2016 District Vice President, District 4, Women's Council of Realtors® , California State
- Business Network International, Referral Solutions Chapter
- Board of Directors, Friends of the Rialto Theater

I Chose a Positive Career in a Beautiful Area

By Duarte A. Teixeira

As a collegian confronted by the need to select a major and minor, and like most other students my age, I was inspired at the thought of a career choice which would enable me to be of service to others. Having explored various majors and minors, I felt drawn to a pre-med major with a business minor. I knew that I wanted my talents to benefit others and at the same time provide well- being for myself and family. I was convinced that medicine was for me, but my interest in the business world began to bloom even as I pursued and completed the math and science curriculum required for this major. It was the sunset of my pre-med major and a brilliant dawn for my business minor.

So what was the deciding factor? Let me be breathtakingly honest with you, Reader, it was a tough decision because my head and my heart were at odds and my hypersensitivity to the pain and suffering of others convinced me that of the two paths, I was best suited for a career in the business world.

I began my real estate career in 1978 by successfully completing requirements for a real estate sales license. Upon completion of additional course work and other requirements, I successfully earned a California real estate broker's license in 1981. Looking back, that seems a long time past, but the energy and enthusiasm that I brought to the profession back then, not only sustained my career, but contributed to the success it became.

My service area is the Northern San Joaquin Valley from Fresno to Sacramento, one of the world's most fertile and productive agricultural regions in the nation, producing 10-12% of the nation's agricultural output. Located a mere one hour drive inland from the San Francisco Bay Area, minutes from Sacramento and a convenient day trip to Yosemite National Park, Lake Tahoe and Reno puts my service area in the very center and heart of the Golden State.

Buyers who have shopped for property in the San Francisco Bay Area are quickly overwhelmed by sticker shock translating to a small house with a big price. Market forces, such as supply and demand, drive home values higher. A major factor driving Bay Area home prices is scarcity. Limited selection drives Bay Area home prices towards seven figures enabling only high earners the ultimate selection. For the average family, the choice is to look elsewhere and that's where I come in. The average buyer is concerned with "bang for the buck" and I've got it.

Beyond affordability, most buyers select my market area for other reasons such as outdoor living. For those who enjoy water sports, there is a network of lakes a short drive away, and many homes come with a swimming pool or sufficient area for building one. The Sierra Nevada mountains are a draw for winter sports including skiing, snow-boarding and family fun in the snow. They are also a magnet for big game hunters while the lakes and rivers draw hunters seeking water fowl and anglers hoping to net a trophy trout, bass or other game fish.

Diverse Real Estate Business

The scope of my business is not merely residential real estate but extends to agricultural, commercial, industrial and other income producing properties. My market area includes a great variety of property types. My specialty is representing either buyers or sellers;

internalizing their goals and making their goals my own. Being fluent in Spanish and Portuguese as well is particularly helpful in assisting clients whose primary language may not be English.

As a kid in school, teachers called me a "book worm" because I loved to read and attack research assignments with enthusiasm. School was a happy place for a kid like me and remains the same today. Perhaps that accounts for the fact that unlike 95% of real estate professionals I earned a college degree in real estate. In addition, I continue to take legal courses including certification of completion in real estate mediation from Pepperdine University School of Law, Straus Institute for Dispute Resolution. I also completed a Certified Negotiation Expert® course along with e-PRO® designation from the National Association of Realtors®. Each transaction is the result of skill and negotiation in behalf of my clients.

Being professional means commitment to the profession itself, colleagues and the clients I serve.

I am involved in local, state and national professional associations, holding membership in my local Association of Realtors® as well as California and National Associations. My peers elected me to the office of association director, state director, and incoming president for the Lodi Association of Realtors®. Simply stated my view is that being professional means being involved.

Is It Location, Location, Location! Or Something Else?

When it comes to buying real estate, the old saying is, "location, location, location!" As important as location however, is the condition of the property. Obsolescence assumes many forms from something as easily recognized and corrected as colors, carpets and appliances to the condition of the roof and sub-area. Nearby properties may also have an influence, not only on value but on desirability. Therefore prudent buyers know that you can never inspect too much. Examine the property completely, walking across the street to form an opinion of "curb appeal". Do you like what you see?

Again, location is an important factor, but what's the most important factor to you? Is it affordability or perhaps school district or maybe proximity to shopping or is freeway access important? Let me caution you to avoid buying the most expensive house in the neighborhood. Prudent buyers know that the "best buy" is not a high value house on the lower value block. Surrounding properties always influence both value and desirability in resale. Hence the home should be of average value, size and appearance of neighboring properties. A high valued property in a neighborhood of lower valued properties seeks the level of the lower values.

So let's decide what's best for you: Is it "location, location, location", or something else? But wait before you reply because I'm about to share with you a trade secret. Think about the sun for just a moment. We know it travels in an orb from east to west and its presence or absence determines what we might do that day. Do you want a sunny or a shady yard, how about a pool or growing your own vegetables? Sunshine is important for outdoor living and that means a western exposure. Valley weather is warm and a shady patio might be just the right thing for you. Which direction does the house face? Are the big windows facing west where the sun will be beating down on that glass all day? Don't forget the sun, it will be important later on.

Like cars, homes come in new or used condition. As real estate professionals we use the term "resale" for any property that has been previously sold or occupied. Each has advantages unique to itself. New construction for example, comes with builder and home component warranties. Resale homes have the advantage of completed landscape and installation of window coverings, each of which is a costly ad-on for a brand new home. National indemnity companies offer various warranties for resale homes reducing the potential risk of costly repairs for the buyer.

Considering new or used, I recommend buyers consider such issues as the expense and time commitment in landscaping a yard. Remember that if you are not a do-it-yourselfer, the cost of installing a yard and sprinklers can be added to the purchase price of the house. Is it still a good buy? We are fortunate that our Valley market offers a wide selection of brand new as well as homes 3-10 years of age.

Financing Matters

Except for the interest rate, the best advice I can give on financing a property is to compare the fees and expenses you are going to incur with that specific loan. A broad variety of loan structures is available for the purchase of a home. The economic meltdown the world recently experienced brought about widespread restructuring of qualifications necessary to obtain a loan. In fact, immediately after the economic meltdown, it was nearly impossible to acquire a loan. Financial institutions tightened their underwriting requirements making it very difficult for some buyers to qualify. Fortunately for all of us, that time has passed and institutions are anxious to make loans to qualified buyers.

One can not understate the importance of preparing financially to make a real estate purchase. Buyers should make an analysis of their income and expenses before looking at property. Car payments, charge card balances and other consumer debt tend to inhibit a buyer's ability to qualify. Contacting a lender well in advance to get pre-approval is one of the initial services I extend to all of my buyers. Together we identify the best program for each buyer, whether it be a conventional loan or a government insured loan such as FHA or VA. To accomplish this I personally escort my clients to well established, reputable lenders to begin the process.

Did you know there is a difference between a mortgage broker and a mortgage banker? Mortgage bankers such as Wells Fargo Bank or Bank of America, lend funds from their portfolio. Unlike a mortgage banker, a mortgage broker, such as 'XYZ Mortgage Inc.' has a multiplicity of sources in which to place the loan sometimes making the process easier. Another source for some buyers is the benefit of membership in a credit union. It's important to determine the best interest rate and costs for acquiring the loan.

My experience is that mortgage brokers can be more flexible when considering an applicant with less than perfect credit. Mortgage brokers sometimes appear able to facilitate remedies for the improvement of blemished credit. Unlike bankers, they have more programs and more solutions for applicants experiencing credit issues. Bankers are typically more regulated, stringent and institutional.

Mortgage brokers and bankers serve their own unique places in the industry. Between lenders, big differences can occur on the out of pocket costs. You need to know what is being charged. I recommend analyzing the different lenders offerings in order to determine your preferred choice.

Selling Your Home Quickly

Location, terms, and property condition dictate how to price a property to sell. Generally, the condition of a property and the terms offered are two important aspects that the seller can control. Apart from sellers control is both location and market conditions. The best price, terms and location will lead to the quickest sale. "Move-in condition" is a genuine buyer motivator because moving is an exhausting, disruptive experience even for the most organized family.

I've learned over the years that convenience and ease of use are as important in buying a home as they are in buying a "gadget". Actually I don't show homes, I demonstrate them. Most agents think buyers are preoccupied with a home's features, but I learned three decades ago that buyers really want benefits. For example it's nice to have double ovens, a great feature actually, but self-cleaning ovens are a greater benefit. Which is more important, the feature or the benefit? Or take the two car garage for example, is there enough room for the hobbyist, car enthusiast or even kids' toys? A two car garage is a nice feature, but does its space provide the benefit you seek?

I advise my sellers to prepare their property well for presentation to buyers. Buyers are quick to make note of shabby or soiled carpet, damaged walls, and generally deferred maintenance. The truth is they don't want to have to clean the house or make repairs before occupying. Painting, organizing, and staging the property is very important. When buyers visit a home personalized with an abundance of family pictures, wall art, figurines and collections of one sort or another, they fail to see the features and benefits the home provides. Make the home as neutral as possible by removing the clutter, using neutral paint colors, cleaning the carpets, neutralizing pet odors, maximize the light by opening up window coverings, cleaning the yard, fixing broken fence boards, etc. Note well that a home in tiptop shape will sell faster and for a better price than its competition.

Value vs. Price

It is exceptionally important not to overprice a home. You perform a great disservice for yourself by overpricing the property. Let me share with you perhaps the most important concept a seller must consider: How much shall I ask for my home? Some sellers answer that question by stating what they need. Now ask yourself a simple question: Do buyers really care about my needs? Your answer will explain the difference between the price to you and the value to your buyers. Need based pricing seldom sells homes. To the contrary, value based pricing supported by comparing the recent sale of similar properties will convince buyers to go ahead with their purchase. And don't forget that an appraiser is not concerned with seller's needs and will soon be employed to verify value for the benefit of both buyer and lender. If the appraisal is less than the contract price, a prudent buyer will be reluctant to proceed in completing the purchase, causing the seller either to lower the price or lose the sale. So, there really is a big difference between price and value and the prudent seller will establish a sales price based on real value as opposed to needs and emotions. This accounts for the failure of most sellers who try to sell without the assistance of a real estate professional.

Buyers choose from alternatives which not only includes size and location but also loan amount, monthly investment plus taxes and insurance. Sellers always want top price and buyers always want the best buy. Smart buyers walk away and look for a similar home for less money, taking the relevant steps to acquire the competitive property instead. You will actually enable the competition to sell because a lower price means a better deal. You will generate more offers if you are at or slightly below market value. Having a professional, a Realtor® who is well-trained, can assist you in determining the exact market value to bring you offers.

I've Decided To Sell, Now What?

Now what? Well, that depends on whether you are looking for the adventure of a "for-sale-by-owner" in uncharted territory or the experienced professional guidance of a relaxing voyage through the well planned steps from listing to marketing, selling, closing and going on with your life. Let's turn our consideration now to some of the relevant steps in successfully selling your home.

Exposure is the elephant in the room. I learned as a kid in school that the letter "A" represents excellence. For a buyer, we've already learned that the letter "A" stands for affordability. For the agent selling your home, the letter "A" stands for availability, meaning that it is always accessible and available for the convenient presentation to buyers. Certain tools we professionals utilize include installation of a distinctive yard sign announcing that your home is available for purchase. This is a valuable tool because experience has shown that oftentimes neighbors have family, friends or associates that are anxious to live in your area. Before a sign is installed and before advertising the property for sale, much preparation is required on the part of the seller. We have already considered the overall appearance of the interior. Now we focus on the exterior.

Your yard need not be the Garden of Eden, but it must be organized and well maintained. This means lawns green and mowed, flowers blooming and dead-headed where necessary, trees pruned etc. Buyers expect strong fences and clean garages. Leaning fences need support, dirty garage floors need cleaning. Oil drips, spills, or grease need immediate attention. Are the gutters of the roof in good repair, meaning without rust or leaks? Don't overlook them. A house in need of exterior paint spells additional cost for a buyer. It is preferable to touch up the paint before the sign is installed. Buyer's first impression begins with the appearance of the entry and surrounding area. The front door area must proclaim loudly to the buyer that this home provides a warm, welcoming, safe and secure experience.

Flooring is also very important, clean carpets are mandatory. Let me give you a tip: As important as fresh paint is your choice of color. Surveys have shown that darker colors make rooms appear smaller while brighter colors tend to make them appear larger. Intense shades of color tend to be quite personal and not appreciated by the majority of buyers. Earth tones are generally acceptable but neutral is the rule of the day. Inspect your cabinet doors and if they show wear, apply products available at all home improvement stores. Because there is so much more to consider, I provide my sellers with printed guidelines on careful preparation so they need not ask, "I've decided to sell, now what?"

Being Professional Means...

When someone asks me; "which is better – employing a Realtor® or selling the home myself?" An easy reply, always on the tip of my tongue, is asking them in return, "Have you studied marketing in college?" Or perhaps I'll ask how many homes have you marketed in the past and what were your results? I am quick to recognize individual differences and proficiencies necessary for the successful marketing, sale and steps to close of escrow. I recognize and applaud seller competencies which might enable me as their agent, to unbundle certain fees for service. "Free" is always best, but everyone loves a discount. The correct answer of course, is that the guidance of professional having a wealth of both education and experience is a better choice than going at it alone.

The number one investment that most people make is the purchase of a home. Protecting that investment ought to be their number one priority; it certainly is my number one goal. Did you know that California real estate law has established 30-40 pages of documentation that the seller must review and execute? That's only the beginning. Clients can expect a volume of over an additional 100 pages before the close of escrow. Smart sellers know they require someone who is competent, trained and has the professional skills to successfully complete the transaction. Consider this: The uninformed "For Sale By Owner" (FSBO) who might fail to execute a required document, although unintentional, risks not only the failure of the sale itself, but also consequences from the operation of law.

So the overall picture of why you should seek out a Realtor® to assist with the sale of your property is that Realtors® have a duty to represent the best interests of all parties. We coordinate a myriad of required appointments, inspections and other events resulting in top dollar with the least inconvenience for the parties.

Your professional agent is the conduit through which all contacts will flow and there will be no shortage of contacts in person, by telephone, email, text, fax, etc. Having a single point of contact is a great convenience for busy sellers, don't you agree? Remember we connect you with trusted partners like inspection companies, title companies, lenders, appraisers and other professional services. We guide you through the entire closing process. We will help you to remain objective so you do not make emotional decisions.

Selecting an agent in whom you have confidence and with whom you feel comfortable is your first major decision. Let's be honest here! Personality is as important as character because you and the agent must be comfortable and communicate easily and effectively. The agent-candidate's age, personality and gender are important considerations for most clients. Some clients will work more effectively with ladies and others with gentlemen. Some sources say that age is related to maturity and a person's outward behavior should reflect both age and maturity. While good humor is very important, bear in mind that while everyone loves a clown, no one follows his leadership.

When choosing an agent, the initial contact is very important. Make note of the time lapse between your initial contact and the agent's response. Did you receive a warm and welcoming reply in a timely manner? Failure to respond quickly from the beginning, might signal what to expect in the future. A foundation stone of real estate practice states: "Time is of the essence" thus being professional means being punctual. The next contact should be a face to face interview with the agent-candidate. Some sellers mistakenly select the first agent they contact. Wise sellers however will interview at least three full-time, active agents in their market.

Part-time or full time, which agent do you think is the real professional? Would you for example, be impressed with an agent who was employed as an auto mechanic five days of the week and attempts to practice real estate in the remaining two days? Better yet, would you trust a medic to perform surgery on you who is only available on weekends because he/she delivers mail in the remaining five days? I believe that time represents commitment and we are really considering herein, the conflict between partial and total commitment. A full time agent is totally committed to client service and success.

Wise sellers prepare well for the initial agent-candidate interview. Here are some guidelines which help in the selection of the successful candidate:

- Please describe your education and experience.
- Please describe your office and support staff, how will they benefit me?
- Will you always be my single point of contact or will I be routed to assistants, secretaries or support staff even though I only hire you?
- Beyond your fee for service or commission, are there other fees charged by you or your firm?

- What will you do to make this entire process simple for me, the consumer?
- What makes you better than most agents?

Honesty is not merely the best policy, it's the only policy for there is none other. The term Realtor® defines that agent's membership in the National Association of Realtors®. Members are required to adhere to the strictly enforced Code of Ethics, copies of which I gladly provide clients upon request. This enables them to see the foundation and framework upon which I have built my professional real estate practice. They appreciate that and I do too!

Technology is a tool not the user's master; being professional means being at ease utilizing the latest technology. Tools such as smartphones, wireless communications, social media, and digital signatures are used daily in my practice. Agents who do not know how to utilize these tools are behind the technological curve and may have difficulty in the conduct of your transaction.

Let Me Tell You How I Work

This is a brief recital of the process describing how I work for you. The longer I am in real estate the more I have determined that no one is neutral on the subject of an open house. Some sellers do not want a parade of strangers marching through their home while others consider it an opportunity to capture buyers. My experience and national surveys confirm year after year the truth that, while an open house provides leads for the agent, it seldom results in the sale of the subject property less than 1% of the time. I will hold an open house upon seller request, however I always inform my sellers that the prospect of a sale resulting from an open house is negligible.

- Pre-listing activities include research and analysis of competing properties offered for sale as well as those which successfully sold and closed and those that failed. This takes place at a face to face conference in which my client has the opportunity to share concerns. It is important to review those properties which failed to sell and examine the reasons for their failure.

- Once I am employed to sell the home, I schedule a secondary conference to review aspects affecting title, existing finance if any and terms of loan payoff. Should the home be located in a planned development having a homeowner's association (HOA) we review restrictions which may involve signage and marketing exposure limitations or restrictions.
- The next step it to submit the property details to the Multiple Listing Service database. All the information I have obtained is entered into the computer and shared with other Realtors®. Placing the property in the Multiple Listing Service announces to the entire membership that a new opportunity exists for their buyers.
- Once offers are received, I prepare net sheets for the consideration of the seller. I explain the buyer's financialposition including available cash, strength of buyer's credit and timeline for closing the sale. At this point I facilitate the seller's decision to accept, reject or submit a counter offer to the buyer.
- Upon final acceptance, the property is pending and the escrow period begins. I now proceed to facilitate the opening of escrow, review of title documents, order the required inspections, accommodate the appraiser, schedule repairs if any, and at every step of the way informing my client of the progress to date.
- Prior to closing I remain in contact first and foremost with clients, the holder of the escrow, lenders, other agents if any, to ensure all documents and disclosures are signed, the property has appraised to value, and the property is ready to close and record on schedule.

Skill in negotiation means greater profit for whomever I represent. A wide chasm exists between negotiating and selling. I prefer to negotiate because it creates a win-win experience for all parties in the transaction. While in selling, you are trying to induce a buyer to go ahead with the purchase. Ultimately you are negotiating interests, priorities, strengths, options and value in an agreement. Understanding the needs or desires of the other party is important. Exploring every option is an element I use to satisfy each party and thereby am able to obtain the most value for my clients. By utilizing these proven negotiation techniques I often save my clients tens of thousands of dollars. Perhaps that accounts for the volume of repeat business as well as referral business that I have enjoyed over my 36+ years of successful real estate practice. Looking back it seems a long time but year after year...there must be a reason.

The End Is Just The Beginning

The end is just the beginning of life happily lived after a successful sale. Presenting the keys to the new buyer is a thrill mutually enjoyed by clients and agent alike. Removing the sign is the mark of success and I've earned the right to ask for referrals. That's a great day indeed.

In the beginning preparing the property is probably the most important thing a seller can do to create buyer interest. But don't forget while you may think price, the buyer thinks value. Those two things will go a long way in helping your agent become a maximum performer. If you, as a buyer or seller, try to veer too much away from the suggestions of your Realtor®, you will end up sabotaging the sale or marketing of your home.

About the Author

Duarte A. Teixeira

Allstar Properties
1219 'E' Street
Modesto, CA 95354

Phone: 209.604.5007
Website: www.ecalprop.com

Wise consumers know that location is often the deciding factor when evaluating real property for purchase. They also know that the education and experience of an agent is the deciding factor for choosing a real estate professional. After thirty-five years of listing and selling all classifications of real property, of owning and managing real estate firms, Duarte A. Teixeira through education and experience has become a leader in his real estate market. In recognition of such, he is now president-elect of his local Association of Realtors® .

Education beyond college graduation is important so Duarte completed required courses for a real estate sales license and then the required courses for a California Brokers License. Achievement in the real estate industry is very important and Duarte has earned certificates as a negotiation expert and real-estate e-PRO® expert. His career long membership in the California Association of Realtors® has led to service in that organization as a state director. He has long served his local association as chairman of various committees and director. He was recently honored with a scholarship to attend and earn a mediator's certificate from the prestigious and world-renowned Straus Institute for Dispute Resolution at Pepperdine University School of Law.

Being professional in an industry in which most consumers make the greatest investment of their lifetime requires well rounded experience beyond merely listing and selling single family homes. Life in the San Joaquin Valley has brought vast experience to this real estate professional in the marketing of multi-unit investments, business opportunities, farms and ranches as well as property management.

A personality with great "people skills" assures wise consumers that they will benefit equally from his education and experience. Most importantly, they are assured of the utmost professional care. With integrity, honesty, loyalty, and with the ultimate goal of exceeding his client's expectations by total commitment to producing results, for Duarte, a commitment isn't a commitment until it is kept.

How I Help My Clients Buy and Sell in Two Different Counties

By Denise Aquila

Like many people, real estate was a second career for me. Prior to real estate, I did consulting for Mid- to Hi-tech firms in Silicon Valley for a number of years. It was very challenging but it was in line with my degree in Business Administration and I enjoyed it very much. However, after some time, the gentleman I was working for decided he was going to retire and suggested that I take over the business. After much consideration I decided that I was not able to do that because I had young children and it really would not work for our family.

At the time I had a very good friend who owned a real estate company, and since I had always been interested in real estate and had bought and sold properties, she encouraged me to get my real estate license. At first I was worried that I wouldn't be able to do it because I am not a salesperson; however, she convinced me that that was precisely why I should do it. She explained to me that selling real estate is not about being a salesperson. It's about being a facilitator. And I thought, "Well, that I can do." I'm really good at putting people together, solving problems and helping people get from point A to point B. My husband and I talked about it. And then he said, "Well, you've always loved real estate. We have invested in our own rental properties. You've helped your family. Why don't you give it a try?" And so, ergo, I started my career in real estate over 23 years ago.

Having a strong business background and working as a consultant has been very beneficial to both me as well as my clients. There was one company I worked with that we actually grew to the point where we took it public on the Stock Exchange. There are so many 'crossing T's and dotting I's" that it really gave me an advantage in real estate. I take real estate very seriously and I don't just whimsically say, "Let's sell you a house and hope it works." I put more of a business angle to it. Yes, a home is a home but it's also the biggest investment of most people's lives. It needs to be something that works for them on all levels.

I don't know very many other Realtors® that approach buying and selling the way I do. For example, I recently had a seller who was interviewing multiple agents and they really wanted a particular price for the house. I loved their house and I said, "I have no doubt, if you list with me, I can sell it. But I cannot get you that price." "Why not?" they asked. I explained to them about the market in relation to their price point they wanted. They said, "Well, is the market going up?" "Yes it is." "What if we waited another year?" I said, "Okay, let's assume you wait another year and let's assume the appreciation rate is X. How much is your monthly payment?" They told me. I said, "Ok, how much is your homeowner's insurance?" They told me. And I said, "What are your taxes?" They told me. So I said to them, "If you keep this house another year, it's going to cost you $36,000 to do that. But you're not going to get $36,000 in appreciation in that period of time. Additionally where you're going, the prices are going to continue to go up because you're going from this market to a different market that's much more robust. So you're actually losing ground in that regard too." Then I said, "Does it really make sense for you to hold out for this particular price?" And they said, "No!" So we listed it and got it sold. He looked at me when I finished and said, "We've talked to other Realtors® and there wasn't a single one that even brought any of that into the conversation."

In 23 years of doing business, there are less than ten people that I've helped during that time who haven't used me for other transactions. I keep track of everything, and they're always pleasantly surprised by that. I really believe in what I do.

Working in Two Communities

When I started my real estate career, my husband and I lived in the Bay area and I was working in San Mateo county. Ten years ago my husband retired and he really did not want to stay in the Bay area so we built a home in Folsom, California, which is a suburb of Sacramento. It is 140 miles away from my real estate office in the Bay area. I wasn't quite sure what I was going to do, and we just thought, "Well, we'll just play this by ear and see how it shakes out." It just so happens that I am still working in both areas ten years later. I started connecting with high school and college classmates that I knew in Sacramento. The next thing I knew, they were calling and asking if I could help sell their parents' homes because they were going into long term care or selling their own homes because they were retiring. It was all word of mouth and it just started snowballing from there. The more time I was spending up in Sacramento where I was living part of the time, the more people started finding out that I sold real estate and I started getting referrals from people I knew from the gym and had met through various organizations. So then the question became: Okay, how am I going to make this work? I tried keeping the two markets separated because there's a big difference between the way real estate is done in Sacramento Valley versus the way it's done in Silicon Valley. Then I noticed something very interesting happen. People in the Bay area were finding out that I was selling up in the Sacramento area as well, and they started approaching me, saying, "We're selling our home here and we want to move there. Can you help us?" The next thing I knew, I was the go-to person for people that were leaving the Bay area and moving to the Sacramento Valley. Then other Realtors® began finding out, and I started getting referrals.

Giving Back to My Community

I played competitive women's soccer until I was 52 years old. I am the type of person that if I find a hole or I find something I'm really passionate about, I think, "Okay, let's make it happen." When my kids were younger, I discovered that there was no organized soccer program for kids. They had different clubs that came in and out and you never knew what was happening; the rules were one way one week and the next way another week. So, I brought AYSO soccer here and I was the first regional commissioner they had. By the time I left, there were over 800 kids playing every summer! Because I was enthusiastic about soccer, so were both our kids. They wanted to continue playing soccer, but the local high school had no women's program. So, I got a petition together and approached the principal and the school board and said, "Look, we need a women's soccer program here. You have the men's but you don't have the women's." The next thing I know, we had soccer at the high school and I was blessed to be the varsity coach for nine years.

In addition to soccer, I was also on the board for CORA, which is Community Overcoming Relationship Abuse, very active in Methodist Church as well as the organized side of real estate. I have to admit I was very surprised to be awarded the Entrepreneur of the Year in 2012 in Sacramento. Honestly I think the reason I won was because people still can't figure out how I balance working in two counties at the same time. In 2005 I was named Realtor® of the Year then in 2006, I was actually the Community Service Award winner for the county, which recognized all the volunteer work that I did. Again, I didn't even know I was up for it. And to put the coup de gras on top of that, in 2010 I was inaugurated into the Bay area Women's Hall of Fame. That was quite the honor as well. I've been very blessed.

The Top Things to Keep in Mind When Buying a Home

When looking for a home, it should be something that you like and it should be in an area that you feel comfortable in. You need to have a clear vision of what you want so you don't get sidetracked. It's also very important to have trust in the agent that you choose to work with to guide you, because you don't do this every day. It's similar to the experience when you go and buy a new car. All of a sudden you see a million of those same cars on the road. When you go to buy a house, all of a sudden, every other person you know has advice for you, whether it's right or wrong. The last thing to keep in mind is that you should never feel like you should buy something more than you can afford. For example, even if your lender says you can afford up to

$500,000, you need to ask yourself how it will feel to make those payments. That's what matters.

What If I Need to Sell my Home Quickly?

If you need to sell your home quickly, the first thing to realize is that it's a business transaction and you need to remove the emotions from it. Over the years I've seen sellers get too fixated on their price. Sometimes you can lose the deal over a matter of a few thousand dollars. Secondly, clear out the clutter. You must depersonalize the house because if someone walks in the door and all they see is your family pictures everywhere, subconsciously they're thinking, "I'm displacing these people if I buy their home." They may not be thinking that on a conscious level but subconsciously they are, and that really will deter someone from purchasing your house. You have to change it from a home to a house and you do this by depersonalizing it. The buyer wants the opportunity to walk around and mentally place their furniture in the bedroom or the living room or see their kids in the kitchen or at the dining room table. And the only way they can do that is if it's a house. If it's a home, it gives the feeling of "This is my house, not yours. Lastly, you must absolutely be prepared for what is going to happen and be realistic about the whole thing.

The Importance of Inspections

During a transaction, depending on what has been provided by the seller to the buyer, the buyer always has the opportunity to do inspections. Sometimes when they get the inspections done, it's a shock to everybody. There might be termite damage, or dry rot, or some sort of problem with the property that the seller didn't even know to disclose because they weren't aware of it. But once the buyer has discovered it, even though you've agreed on a particular price for the house, the buyer is likely going to want to renegotiate.

Recently I had a transaction for a buyer where the house looked absolutely gorgeous when you walked through. It looked very well maintained; it was impeccable. We did a termite report, which doesn't just mean the presence of termites. It also looks for active damage to the property due to water leaks or anything like that. The termite report indicated that there was $1,300 worth of damage that needed to be taken care of. Further, the home inspection discovered lot of other little things that added up to about $7,000-$8,000 of repairs. I sat down with the buyer and said, "Okay, these things are really important to fix. Although you could probably do some of them later, they are going to cost you money. So what would you like to do with this?" She made a list of the repairs that she wanted done and we sent that back to the seller. Now the seller's already thinking, "I'm getting X number of dollars for my house." The buyer is thinking she's going to move into a house that she doesn't have to do repairs on because it looked like it was in such great shape. And all of a sudden, the inspections tell you otherwise. In these situations, we try to strike a happy medium. Ultimately we were able to say, "Okay, let's split the difference. You pay $2,500 more Mr. Buyer and Mr. Seller, you take $2,500 less. And we close next week as planned." So we were able to work it out.

Staying Connected

I had clients once, who were not really ready to buy but they were referred to me so I thought I would show them around and get an idea of what they liked. We spent three or four weekends looking at properties. I knew they both had really good jobs, so I wasn't worried about them getting approved for financing. But what I didn't know was that they had some school debt that had to be paid off. At one point I told them to get the financing piece done so we could see what they could afford. That's when we realized that they weren't in a position to buy right away because they had to get a little bit more of their debt paid off. Over time, I was communicating with them but then they moved from one apartment to another and I had changed companies so we lost track of each other.

A few years later, I was holding an Open House. I was in the dining room talking to a couple that had come to see the house and we were laughing about something. It turns out that they were in another room and heard me laughing. They looked at each other and said, "Oh my goodness, that's Denise!" Anyway, they realized it was me and they came into the dining room saying, "Oh my goodness, Denise, we've found you!" It was like old home week, it was the funniest thing. Two months later, I had them in a house. We are still friends to this day. We have dinner together regularly and we've even vacationed together.

They've become like family and it was just so funny how we reconnected again at a house I was trying to sell!

How I Market a New Listing

Every marketing plan that I have for every home is different. People say, "Well, how do you make them different? You put it in the MLS, you do flyers, you do this, you do that." A lot of it is the same, of course, but I do create a comprehensive marketing program for each individual house. Some houses lend themselves to having multiple open houses. Other houses, because of where they're located or other circumstances may not make sense to have open houses. I've had people tell me before that they didn't want pictures on the Internet of bedrooms of their homes because they feel like it's an invasion of their privacy. So I have to market a little bit differently if I have a seller that has certain wishes or desires.

I have not done print advertising in years, but I spend a lot of my marketing budget to ensure that the house is marketed well on the Internet. For example, each listing goes on no less than thirty different websites. It goes all over the country. It goes everywhere. That's worth its weight in gold.

How to Increase The Value of Your Home

To increase the value of your home, the first thing to do is to create great curb appeal. If you can't get them in the front door, it doesn't matter how fabulous your house is, they'll never see it. Make sure the lawn is mowed. Plant some flowers, even it's just setting them in pots and placing them around to create some color out front. Make it inviting. Often I tell people to paint their front door. Curb appeal is really and truly the most important thing because it doesn't matter if you've got fabulous granite and beautiful hardwood floors if you can't even get them to come through the front door.

The second most important thing is what I mentioned earlier – decluttering your house. Make it a blank slate that someone else can see themselves in and they'll be more likely to pay you what you want. Try to make it look big and spacious. Make sure the curtains are open so you have lots of natural light coming in so that it feels warm and inviting. And then the last thing, which is probably one of the most important, is to take care of any deferred maintenance that you can. People don't mind having older countertops or older cupboards if it's clean and it looks nice. But if your fence is falling down or there are obvious things that need to be repaired, you should get those taken care of.

Once potential buyers come in and start picking on one thing, it's easy to pick on a lot of things. I often tell my clients when we're preparing their home for sale all the things I need them to do. I'll literally go in and I'll say, "We need to paint. I want you to paint the rooms." Or, "I want new carpet put in here." If I'm asking them to spend $5,000 to do work on the house, my expectation is that I'm going to get them $10,000 of added value. If I can't get them more than they're putting in, what's the point?

If you want to get the maximum asking price for your home, preparing your home is critical.

The Benefits of Using a Realtor®

If you use a Realtor® to sell your home, there's a very good chance that you'll get more money than trying to do it yourself. That's actually a proven fact. It's tracked year in and year out by data companies that look at the real estate market, track which homes sells, at what price and how long it is on the market. Realtors® simply get more money for the home than a For Sale By Owner does. Even though they think they will save money, they often end up costing themselves money. Also, by using a Realtor® you get a lot more visibility for your house, so you have a lot more potential buyers. If you're a For Sale By Owner, someone may not even know your house is for sale. It may be the perfect house for them, but if they don't happen to drive by that particular time when you have your For Sale sign out, they may never even see it.

In addition, real estate agents, or Realtors®, are professionals and a homeowner is not. And your chances of being sued once you've sold your home are much less if you've used a Realtor® than if you try it on your own. You may have great intentions as a homeowner and you may fill out paperwork or disclose what you think is important, but if you close escrow on that house and your water heater explodes two or three months after you've closed, guess what that buyer's going to do? They're going to come to you as the seller and say, "You didn't tell me that hot water heater wasn't working properly, or that it had a problem. And now, it ruined something in my garage because it exploded so now I'm going to sue you." You may not have a leg to stand on. If you used a Realtor®, you could go back to the Realtor® and say, "Did we do the proper disclosures?" And if you did, then you don't need to worry. Probably the biggest thing is the homeowner can't protect themselves enough. They may think they can but they really and truly can't. That's why we have so many rules and regulations and we take continuing education all the time.

Why Communication Matters

In terms of communication between Realtor® and client, three things come to mind. The first one is Honesty. Buyers and sellers need their agent to be honest with them. I tell all my clients, "I'm going to tell you the good, the bad, and the ugly and some of it you may not want to hear but I'm going to tell you anyway because they need to know." Whenever there's a showing, I always call the agent and ask for feedback. Then, once a week I sit down and call or email my clients, and say, "In the past seven days, your home has been shown this many times. This has been the response from the agents. We're not expecting an offer. The reason is it either didn't work because of the floor plan or they felt the house was too much money or X." They may not want to know that someone thinks the house is too much money but they need to know that so when we do get an offer, if it's not the price they wanted, they've got the background that they've had twenty other people look at it and have said, "No" because it either didn't work for them or the price wasn't right. So that gives them ammunition to make a good decision. They really need to expect honesty from their agent.

Communication is critical. You've got to have open communication and it's got to be both ways. I always tell my sellers that if they feel uncomfortable about something I'm doing, don't just talk about it at pillow talk. Call me so we can get together and have a discussion about it. If it's something that I'm clearly forgetting to do or it's something important to them that they didn't voice to me or that I'm not aware of, I'm happy to do it. But let's talk about it first.

Lastly, buyers and sellers really should expect the agent to work for them until the job is complete. I've seen it before where listing agents get their sellers in to escrow and then it's like they've fallen off the face of the earth. When my client's home is in escrow, I still communicate with them every week, even if it's just to say, "Inspections are done. I'm waiting to hear from the buyer's agent. I haven't heard anything, we're just waiting to hear." They want to be able to sleep at night. By me working until the end, it gives them more confidence. As an example, I go to all my sign-offs with my buyers and sellers. Now, at that point, my job is done. There really isn't anything for me to do at the title company when they're signing the closing papers or they're signing their loan papers. However, I want them to know I'm there even if they have a question and I can't answer it because it's related to their loan, for example, I'm there to give them support. I'm there with them to the completion of the transaction. And I'm the one that calls them and tells them, "Congratulations, your home is sold. Check your bank account in the next 24 hours and your proceeds are there." Or, "Where am I meeting you to give you your key?" I'm there with them until the very end.

Ongoing Appreciation For My Clients

Even after the house is sold, it's really not the end because I always pop by their houses from time to time. I tailor the closing gifts that I give to my buyers and sellers. They're very rarely ever the same. I try to give them something that makes sense, that they'll use, and every year at Christmas, I always give clients a little something. One year I gave out Christmas ornaments and another year I gave out Christmas candy dishes. This way they think of me at least during the holidays!

I love to cook, and all my clients know I love to cook. Even if I ask them to go out for dinner, they say, "No, no, no, we want you to cook!" Many of my clients have been to my house. One year I did a really fun client appreciation series based around the kitchen. It was so fun because I gave them little gifts every other month. For example, one month they got an egg beater with a little note that said, "Eggstra! Eggstra! Read all about it! Your Realtor® is beating up everybody in town to get you the best deal." And then on the back of the little tag was a recipe that you would have to use an egg beater for. It got to be funny because they were always wondering what was coming next. I also gave away little jar scrapers ("Scraping every last penny out of your real estate transaction for you") and measuring spoons and so on. It was lots of fun. I remember going into Bed, Bath and Beyond and I said to the clerk, "I want to buy sixty of these." She looked at me like I had six eyeballs. She said, "What do you do with that many of them?" So I told her, "I do these little gifts for my clients. I pop by and say hi and I give them a little gift." She replied, "Really? Can I be one of your clients?" And I said, "Certainly. But there's a caveat with that. You either have to buy or sell with me or send me a referral. You do one of those three things and you can be my client." And she actually sent me a referral! We still laugh about that. I am never sure what the day will bring or where my next client will come from.

Happy Buyers and Sellers

Happy buyers and sellers is what I strive for because there's an old saying that says, "If you do a bad job, that person is going to turn around and tell ten people that you've done a bad job." And it may be that, in fact, you did do a bad job. But it may very well be that you didn't. Regardless you can't afford to have that kind of negative rumor going around out there. That's why I always strive to do the very best job that I can to make sure all of my clients are happy. I tell them from the very beginning that my whole goal is to help them achieve what they want and to create a win-win situation for everyone. And it may not be that they get exactly what they want, but if we compromise and everybody is happy in the end, that's the goal.

About the Author

Denise Aquila

Alain Pinel Realtors,
San Mateo and Folsom

Phone: 650-740-8930
Email: denise@deniseaquila.com
Website: www.DeniseAquila.com

For more than 20 years, Denise Aquila has built a reputation as an extraordinary Realtor® with a heart for her clients. By helping them achieve their goals, Denise has become a perennial Top Producer earning numerous accolades over her career, including Rookie of the year and Realtor® of the year.

"I always put the needs of my clients first," she says. "There is no better feeling than helping my clients find the home of their dreams or helping them sell their house and move onto the next chapter of their lives."

For Denise, her commitment starts with listening. "You can't help your clients achieve their goals until you know what their goals are," she says. By starting with one basic question, Denise helps her clients determine exactly what it is they're looking for and what they need from her. "I always ask, "Where do you want to be in five years? In 10 years?" By helping them clearly define their needs, Denise is better prepared to find it for them.

Denise is dedicated to her local community and the industry she loves. She volunteers at multiple local organizations. Because of her dedication to volunteerism she earned the 2006 Community Service Award and was named Entrepreneur of the Year in 2013.

Developing the Art of Listening

By Mark Hoadley

What I really wanted... *Was to Direct.*

Most of the family thought I would end up becoming a lawyer. By the tender age of eight my negotiating skills had become legendary. Without power, without money, even without transportation I made sure we never ran out of Fruit Loops although the suggested morning course was always Shredded Wheat.

I grew up in the sales world. My father owned and operated a small used car dealership during my toddler years. He would eventually become one of the first of three RV Dealers to launch in LA County. He went on to become the fairly well known and highly respected owner of Hoadley Motor Sales in the South Bay Area.

Wally was loved by almost all who encountered him. His customers always came back to him. His employees stayed, even when times where tough. He was an awesome sales-professional. He had a knack for bringing the best out of people - he was really good at it. He was a great Dad and one that I could never get enough of. When it came to working with others and learning about how to build meaningful long-term relationships, I couldn't have had a better teacher. He taught me well in my formative years. We lost him in 1993. I've come to believe that my father had much to do with the success I've experienced as an adult – particularly since he's been gone.

Not only was my Dad my mentor he would become my best friend. He always came up with the best suggestions. I think that's because he was always listening. Wally had developed an outstanding reputation in his industry and with his customers. He taught me that the key to being a successful sales person was effective listening – it's the first step in effective communication.

In my teenage years I'd learned everything there was to know about Recreational Vehicles. We serviced and sold Motor Homes, Campers, & Trailers. I went from lot boy, to service mechanic, to assistant service manager. Eventually I transitioned into a sales position at the dealership as I was working my way through College.

I had spent most of my high school years working in Theater. It started with acting. I appeared in numerous school plays before I got heavily involved working in stagecraft and lighting. Video production was a new medium and really starting to come on big. While attending college I studied photography and spent much of my electoral time working in the newest medium - video production. Soon I was hooked and actively working on school productions. While my sales position at the family business paid the bills, my heart remained with video production because... What I really wanted... Was to Direct. I always knew I was headed for Hollywood.

I was about a year out of College when I was finally able to fulfill my dream and work in Hollywood on a film crew. I started out as an intern for a relatively unknown Cinematographer named Russell Carpenter. My Hollywood journey began working on a feature film called the Wizard of Speed and Time. While the film never quite made it at the box office, I continued to work with Russell on various productions as his assistant. We were using brand new real-time video technology. It involved a sending device that attached to Russell's camera allowing for instant playback of what had just been filmed. After each segment was filmed I usually had Russ and the Director over my shoulder reviewing various "takes" on my field monitor. The hours were long but I learned a lot. It was really an exciting time.

After about a year working with Russ an event occurred that changed everything. I was involved in a serious car accident. An uninsured motorist had broadsided my car. I sustained multiple broken bones including a broken sacrum, a concussion, and prolonged blurred vision from injuries sustained to both eyes. I couldn't lie down or walk for months. I was a real mess. I didn't have health insurance. I did most of my convalescing in a recliner. Medical bills were piling up. The miniscule auto insurance settlement I received didn't quite cover things.

After about the third call from Russell I was still not well enough to work. Eventually the calls stopped coming in. I wouldn't see or hear from Russ again for another 20+ years. It was Oscar Night when I next encountered him. He was on TV. He was walking across the stage to accept the Academy Award for Best Cinematography for his work on Titanic. Needless to say, those long months following the car accident had been a really difficult time.

When I was finally able to get back on my feet again I had amassed a significant amount of debt. I had to figure out how to pay the medical bills I'd accumulated. I also had to take a really hard look at my situation, assess my future, and review my skillset. I needed consistent work that could sustain a decent income. I enjoyed working with people and had already developed strong sales skills from the years I spent working with my father. What could I do? I decided to change course and study Real Estate. I enrolled at the most respected institution I could find on the West Coast – Lumbleau Real Estate School.

Taking a Leap of Faith

It was about this same time that my wife Christine and I decided we were ready to start a family. I knew we couldn't qualify to purchase a suitable property in Los Angeles County so in 1989 we relocated to North San Diego County. We bought our first home in a community called Shadowridge located at Southern end Vista bordering Carlsbad and South Oceanside. By this time I had obtained my License to sell Real Estate. I immediately went to work starting my Real Estate practice at a small office called Shadowridge Realty. I knew no one. I had no referral base, no sphere of influence, nothing. I was green but bold.

We purchased our home in the fall of 1989. It was near the conclusion of a remarkable period when most North County homes had appreciated about 33% in just nine months. This was the actually the pinnacle of an unusual spike in the housing market. I had no idea at the time but I had just chosen to purchase a home and start a career in Real Estate at the beginning of what would become perhaps the most difficult and challenging period ever experienced in the San Diego Real Estate market.

After what had been a hugely speculative period, the San Diego market experienced a slow economically driven depression that would go on to last seven long years. Prices would eventually drop 45 percent. The defense industry in San Diego County, far and away the largest employer, was shutting down. Jobs of all kinds were going away rapidly. Folks packed up and moved to Oregon. Families routinely abandoned their homes, many with underwater mortgages. Folks were leaving their keys on the counter with the note, "gone to Texas". It was a kind of mass exodus. Short Sales, Foreclosures, Auctions - all were the order of the day. Inventory levels eventually grew to roughly 7 times what they are today.

I was completely unprepared at first; the process of getting educated for your Real Estate license does nothing to prepare you for the practical things you need to know about the mechanics of a home sale. But the real difficult test was of course, the market itself. It was steadily cycling downward. Prices were falling. There was little confidence in the market. Transactional volume in the marketplace was steadily dropping and would continue to do so for 5 straight years. By 1994 two-thirds of the San Diego County Real Estate Agents that were practicing in 1989 – had left the industry. You might say I survived the school of hard knocks.

So much has changed since then. For example, when I started in real estate, access to our Multiple Listing Service was reserved only for members – Realtors® and Real Estate Agents. The information belonged to the listing agents, the ones who contracted with sellers to put the information together, they shared it with cooperating agents who were members of our Board and the Multiple Listing Service. It was private information. To become a member of the MLS you had to be a Realtor® or Agent in good standing. The information was produced and compiled by the members and you had to be a member to access it. There was no public access – buyers and sellers had to rely on the MLS members - Realtors® and Agents. There was a lot of work done over the telephone back then, email wasn't happening yet,

I remember when the fax machine made the scene – now that was a big deal!

There were computers but Al Gore had yet to really 'invent" the Internet. We would submit listing information to our Board and within a couple of weeks it would get published in what we called the Blue Book. It was the size of a telephone directory - about three inches thick - printed on very thin newsprint. It was published every two weeks. There were 12 listings displayed on each page, in very fine print. That's what we cooperating Realtors® would use to select properties to show our clients. All the property information was in a very confined little box. There was only one tiny exterior photo of the subject property.

If a change happened to a listing or one needed to happen such as: a price reduction, a change in the terms offered, if the property went pending in-escrow, or if it came off the market - the change would only take effect every two weeks because the Blue Book was only published every two weeks. Oh, and there wasn't any mapping. If you truly wanted to convey any meaningful information about a listing to your client you had to go out and see the property for yourself. You had to find it for yourself too. Thomas Bros published our "Bible" back then.

Where I became successful was working with buyers, especially entry-level buyers. Because there were so many properties listed, and because there was so much inventory to choose from; Realtors®, brokers, and agents were becoming overwhelmed. The few buyers we had exploring the marketplace actually had too many properties to choose from. It was crazy. It seemed impossible to keep up with the new inventory and the constant changes – especially while prices were continuing to fall – buyers remained wary, skeptical, and skittish.

At that time, the primary problem buyers were faced with was that their agents often failed to realize how a particular listing stacked up with the competing inventory (This issue is mitigated today because of the wealth of on-line listing information now instantly available - it makes assessing other available and competing inventory a much easier task). Back then, unless the agent personally previewed all of the competing inventory, it was next to impossible to determine what kind of value was really offered with any given subject property. If there was a road noise detriment or other significant issue affecting a particular property, it often could not be known unless the home was previewed in person. With the daunting number of listings to choose from, a buyer's agent had to have really done their homework to be able to offer sound advice. Buyers in general were already lacking confidence in the market. Put an unprepared agent into the mix and most buyers would quickly second-guess themselves. Listing agents were especially weary due to the high percentage of transactions that tended to fall out of escrow.

I decided to employ a system where I could offer my clients a service they couldn't find anywhere else. Let me explain. The information available on listings was extremely limited, while at the same time, the number of these listings making up our active inventory was skyrocketing. Consequently it was becoming increasingly difficult to differentiate between what might be a good property and what was indeed a Great Property. Active inventory was so voluminous agents had a difficult time keeping track. Eventually most agents simply stopped previewing new listing inventory. Most of the time, the "Buyers Agent" would be seeing the listing for the first time - while they had their buyer in tow – usually during the showing appointment. With the dramatic increase in inventory this practice soon became the new normal.

I was relatively new in the business. In the beginning, having only a few clients at any given time, I wasn't being pulled in dozens of different directions at once. This allowed me the time to commit to good old-fashion footwork at the level other agents either lacked the time for, were unwilling, or unable to do. Back in the day, after painstakingly filtering down the inventory that was presented in the "blue book", it would not be unusual for me to spend 2-3 days driving around previewing 50 or 60+ properties prior to meeting my client. When working with a new buyer that's really what it took to find the very best value and the right fit for the client. Doing this kind of footwork for a number of years also provided me with quite an education. This acquired knowledge of our North County marketplace still comes in handy today.

This practice turned out to be a difference maker. It also encouraged me to become even more effective at the art of listening. Get it wrong - and I could be on a three-day wild goose chase preparing to show my client all the wrong properties. Get it right – and after spending days actively previewing the most suitable inventory - I'd usually only need to show the client one or two homes. After this kind of preparation, I was pretty confident about which listing was going to be the best fit for my client. I soon developed a reputation as a top Buyer's Agent.

Even today, many of my buyer-controlled transactions involve showing the client only one or two properties. A well-educated buyer soon becomes a buyer that knows what they want – when given a choice – they will always want to see the best listing first. These days, because of their ability to access listing information, even buyers that feel pretty confident in their knowledge of the available inventory will usually want to see the best listing available in their price range first. Much like an attorney preparing for a court case, a good Realtor® will listen carefully and take all the necessary steps in preparing for the client. This not only serves the customer, it respects their time, and ultimately - it honors that client. This usually does not go unnoticed.

While so much has to do with asking the right questions of the client, the other 50% is about listening for what's in-between the lines. Every client is different. They cannot always be effectively interviewed in the same way. Finding out about what attributes matter most to the client is the key. Sometimes we don't already have all the right questions in place to effectively determine what matters most to a particular client. This makes listening effectively to everything the client is saying or not saying all the more important.

The art of listening includes carefully observing everything the client is showing us. Oftentimes, it also involves determining what the clients may be hiding (even on a subconscious level) from us, or themselves. It's about observing what they are doing and not doing. Most importantly - it's always about carefully observing how the client is reacting throughout the buying or selling process - and then effectively conveying that important feedback back to them.

I truly believe that doing the difficult footwork while developing this art of listening is really what set me apart during those most difficult early years in the business. Not only did it set me up for future success in the business, I think the experience continues to serve my clients well today. I've always tried to prepare for my clients in a fashion that is not unlike when a good lawyer prepares to present their prepared case in a courtroom. My experience suggest that - after their Offer has been accepted or their Escrow has successfully closed - a Homebuyer or Seller should always feel as if they reached a natural conclusion after witnessing and reviewing all the facts of a well prepared case.

North San Diego County

You'll always be able to find me at NorthCountyHouseHunter.com. I started developing the website over twenty years ago. Today it's home for thousands of folks looking for good information about the area. It's become the Portal to North San Diego County to many a prospective homebuyer and home seller. Folks visiting the site are usually looking for more information about our little slice of heaven - an area that locals mostly refer to as North County.

North San Diego County is the weather capital of the continental United States. It's a diverse area. Along the coast most folks consider North County to begin in Del Mar moving North to Encinitas, Carlsbad, and finally Oceanside. Inland cities include Vista, San Marcos, Fallbrook, Escondido, Rancho Bernardo, and Poway. Some of the cities, like Carlsbad and Oceanside are really diverse and are actually quite large geographically. Generally our cities will have an urban downtown area and suburban neighborhoods. Most of our cities still have rural areas with larger lots, some that allow for nurseries and horses.

North San Diego County has so much going for it. Biotech, Defense, Telecom, Software, Engineering firms, even the Golfing industry, many are all home based here. Our elementary, middle, and high schools are quite excellent. Cal State San Marcos is the newest University in the system. The beaches are a short drive away for most residents. It works well for or people who need to commute. Your average commute time from North County to Downtown San Diego or South Orange County is generally going to be between 30 to 45 minutes.

Buying a Home

I find that buyers of new homes in particular sometimes forget, or are not aware of, one of the most important factors when assessing Real Estate – the real value is in the land. It's easy to do when skilled interior designers and architects are wooing the customer with spectacular architectural features and beautifully staged model homes.

When it comes to value in Real Estate, the key factor to always keep in mind is the land upon which the home sits. That's the only thing that really increases in value over time. People forget that the structure actually depreciates over time. You have to invest in the structure and improve it over the years to keep it up to current standards. There's really very little you can do about the land upon which the home sits. Orientation to the sun, noise, privacy, view all are key factors when assessing value in any given neighborhood.

Experience has taught me that the single most important aspect and typically one of the most desirable features most homebuyers are looking for when considering their next home purchase is privacy. Most folks are not aware that the single best investment anyone can make to improve the value of their real estate is to plant a tree, while always keeping a particular focus on enhancing the privacy of their lot and outdoor living areas.

I'm always very selective when it comes to the lots when presenting properties for my clients' consideration. This doesn't mean we confine our searches to very exclusive or expensive areas. There are plenty of great neighborhoods in some of our more affordable cities like Oceanside, Vista, and San Marcos. Neighborhoods like Santa Fe Hills, Shadowridge, Rancho Del Oro, and Jeffries Ranch – just to name a few - offer outstanding schools, parks, and services. No matter which city or neighborhood my clients are looking at, I'll always point out the lot that offers the most privacy or a property where a private setting can be easily produced with the help of proper vegetation. Not only will this issue always be an important factor when it comes to resale, it will have a large influence on the use and enjoyment of the home.

Hoadley's Top Three…

The top three things a person needs to keep in mind when purchasing a home are:

First: Always remember, the only thing that goes up in value in Real Estate is the land upon which the structure sits. The structure depreciates in value every year and you'll need to pay to maintain it and improve it.

Second: Not only is every home an investment - every home is a money pit, but it will always be your money pit, and not the landlords. Eventually you'll likely recoup your investment and it may perhaps grow substantially - in the meantime you'll have a nice place to live. .

Third: And this is the most important one - NEVER incur debt service on a property that will end up exceeding 25% of what the property can effectively rent for - lest you might find yourself "buried", "underwater", or forced to sell in a bad market. Real Estate does not appreciate in a straight line. You might have an agent tell you your $500,000 investment will soon be worth $600,000. If so - tread carefully. I've seen homes that cost $500K fall in value to the low $300's and settle there for years before they ever effectively appreciate in value. Remember the 1990's? How about 2008-2012?

Should your family suffer in an economic downturn where you can't pay your bills, or you need to relocate for work, or some other catastrophe comes along... You'll want to always have the option to rent-out your property. During a really bad or depressed market you never want to find yourself forced to sell while in the midst of it.

Selling Your Home

It's always a good time to invest in Real Estate. There's never really a bad time to buy because you're going to have the use and enjoyment of the property to live in or raise your family. While there is never really a bad time to buy Real Estate, however, there are going to be really bad times to sell real estate. You never ever want to find yourself in a position where you're forced to sell your home in a bad market.

Every home-seller I've ever met wants to sell their home for the highest possible price, without exception. Most want to net the most possible proceeds and wish to do so in a most effective and efficient manner. It all starts with hiring the very best professional you can find that knows your market. Typically you'll want to hire a Listing Agent who works and lives within a 10 to 12 mile radius of your property. This can really be important because you'll want that agent to be able to easily access the property and they should know the local competing inventory like the back of their hand.

Correctly and competitively (and all markets are competitive) pricing your property is crucial, particularly in the high technology age. If the listing is priced right it will attract a lot of attention. Be sure to find an agent who will do their due diligence and spend time explaining their pricing strategies with you. Pricing the listing correctly will almost always increase the seller's bottom line in the long run and eliminate the often disastrous results of a listing "getting old" in the marketplace. A good listing agent will take the time to carefully explain various pricing strategies and how they work. One that leads to multiple offers, handled by an experienced agent skilled in patiently orchestrating the process, can often lead to an especially good outcome for the seller – not only in terms of the selling price but also in getting other terms that can benefit and assist that seller with the acquisition of their replacement property.

Preparing your home to sell involves staging. Your Realtor® should be able to assist you with this. It doesn't mean that you have to spend a lot of money hiring a professional staging outfit or that you need to refurnish your home. It may mean that, with your Realtor's® guidance (and sometimes his elbow grease), you need to take a couple of weekends and roll up your sleeves. Moving or removing furnishings and/or personal items or perhaps loading some of the family's "stuff" into a temporary storage facility should always be accomplished prior to a property being actively marketed. Beyond de-cluttering and opening up the rooms, it's almost always a good idea to power wash the exterior and get the windows professionally washed. Take a good look at the entryway and front door too. I have a few more tricks up my sleeve but you'll have to hire me to get my best secrets.

Because of my education and because I was so picky, I did my own Real Estate Photography for years. It took some years until I was fortunate enough to find a truly skilled photographer that really knew how to shoot interiors. Today on-line marketing has helped create a cottage industry of very good photographers and videographers. Most home sellers should insist that their agent hire a professional unless he or she can demonstrate their the level of work is on par with qualified photographers that are now widely available.

The Internet is very much in control of our marketing efforts these days. Consumer driven websites have taken over when it comes to marketing homes now. Print advertising is history. Even empty nesters and retirees are getting comfortable searching for listings on-line with their Smart Phones, iPads, and Laptops. It's imperative that your Realtor® is skilled in harnessing the power of this. Presenting a compelling message when marketing the subject property is where it all starts. The "remarks section" in our MLS only allows for 543 characters – that's all that get pulled into most consumer websites - your Realtor® needs to know how to best use this section. This is where I have the opportunity to reach out and get into the head of the on-line home shopper. When I'm preparing this section for my sellers I'm always focusing on verbiage that will compel the suitable buyer to call their agent and set a viewing appointment.

You don't ever want your agent to leave any information out of the listing. Most agents always want to make sure all the fields are covered, every one of them. Never leave anything to chance in terms of how a listing is going to get picked up in a search. There are listing input fields that are not required to be completed in our MLS system yet they're critically important. View, type of view, single level, map coordinates – I've seen all these fields input incorrectly or flat-out omitted. Be sure your agent sends you a full detailed MLS spreadsheet so you can proof the information. Even the great agents make a typo once in a while.

There are many effective ways to get the message out about listings. Technology today makes the competition for the next appropriate buyer fiercer than ever before. Sometimes it helps to think outside the box. For instance, I found that home search engines particularly on larger consumer sites such as Zillow are driven primarily by zip code or the name of a particular city. Specifically for this reason, I decided about ten years ago to change the name of my website to: www. NorthCountyHouseHunter.com. I figured this might help my sellers broadcast their listings in a manner that might be more easily accessed by our North County population - all of whom know the area as and often refer to the area as "North County". Turns out the website title caters to all 3.1M residents of San Diego County because folks that live anywhere in San Diego County are quite familiar with the term "North County". Most use the vernacular regularly. The website presently generates a tremendous amount of additional traffic for my sellers. We're also able to attract homebuyers that might otherwise not be reached – particularly those folks shopping for champagne on a beer budget. Oftentimes our site outperforms Zillow. I'm really kind of proud of that.

Open Houses

If you happen to be in a market that's moving exceptionally fast, open houses can be useful, provided they encourage competing offers. If a Listing Agent wants to hold your home open repeatedly, I would be concerned that the agent might not be as interested in selling your home as they are about building up buyer leads or contacts with your neighbors. Keep in mind that if your listing agent presents you with your only offer, and that offer was procured from their Open House, he or she may not be as passionate about seeing additional competing offers come in on the property, as you might be.

When I thoroughly discuss open houses with sellers, fewer and fewer want to hold them. Many home-sellers realize that with the technology available today, open houses are just not that necessary. Open Houses can tend to benefit the agent more than the homeowner by allowing the agent to meet the neighbors or troll for buyers.

I don't object to other newer agents holding my listings open, it allows them to make contact with potential homebuyers and develop those relationships. Offers procured from an Open House should always be considered provided the listing has been allowed to have its Day in The Sun. I consider this to be a minimum presence of three days actively marketed in the Multiple Listing Service. If the appropriate buyer is active and out there, they will most likely have discovered your listing by then. Generally, if we've had at least 72 hours exposure, I'll be able to alert a prospective buyer's agent that we have an offer and to not delay in throwing their hat in the ring.

If your Realtor® is doing their job correctly, they're bringing your property to market with a compelling message, they're orchestrating an array of on-line resources to target the right buyers, and they're actively engaging with the 20% of the agents out there that are typically selling about 80% of the properties. Hopefully you've hired an agent that belongs in that 20% club.

If you're a Seller that ends up hiring the right Realtor® you have an advantage because your agent has established hundreds of relationships with the very best Realtors® in the industry – each of whom may have one or more potential buyers for your home. Once my seller's listing has been activated in the MLS, the best way for me to invest my time on their behalf, is actively engaging with these same Realtors® - with many of whom I've already established good working relationships. That's how I'm able reach the greatest number of buyers for my sellers.

Brokerage Fees

Sometimes sellers fail to realize the real value of hiring the right Realtor®. Occasionally I'll hear from a seller that says they have a licensed friend or family member who's willing to list their property for half of what I need to charge for the listing side of the commission. What that same home seller typically fails to realize is: the 1-1.5% they think they're saving with this type of agent - will likely to be costing them tens of thousands of dollars more when it comes down to net proceeds they'll realize on the actual selling price of the property. When it comes down to a seller's bottom line – hiring the right Realtor® will almost always net them far more in net proceeds from the sale of their home. Typically a discount broker's or part time licensee's main strength is their ability to cut their fee in half. How's that skill set going to work out when they're negotiating with the equity you have in your home?

A good agent will always strive to earn their fee by increasing their client's bottom line. The right Realtor®: knows how to price the property correctly, is a skilled negotiator, understands how to market the seller's particular type of Real Estate (often because he has done this hundreds of times before), is well known locally, and perhaps most importantly - has developed relationships (often over decades) with the other top producing cooperating agents, the same agents that will likely be representing the buyer of your property.

Since 87% of Real Estate transactions involve a cooperating agent, hiring the right listing agent to represent your interests is hugely important. A real pro is far more attached to the satisfaction and wellbeing of his client than he is to his commission. Typically, a licensee that cuts his or her fee in half has to do twice the sales volume in order to earn a living in this business. Client service and/or the commitment to the clients' wellbeing is most often what's sacrificed in these situations. There simply are not enough hours in the day.

Sellers focused on the brokerage fees often overlook the value of the representation they'll receive when it comes to the escrow process. Licensees lacking in experience, lacking the knowledge, or simply lacking in the skills necessary to successfully close an escrow without any unwanted surprises - often provide unwanted results. These results can sometimes be costly, be disastrous, or just be really painful. With a real pro - the heartburn factor escrows can sometimes produce - is likely to be significantly reduced.

A real pro will not cut their fee in half just to get a listing – they would sooner walk away. Think about it. If you have a life threatening disease do you want a cut-rate doctor? If you are in some kind of real legal trouble, are you going to go to a cut-rate attorney? If a licensee is desperate enough to cut their fee in half, is that someone you want representing you when you're involved in one of life's most important financial endeavors – involving perhaps your largest asset?

A great Realtor® will always keep their clients' best interest in mind and ahead of their own. They'll always be looking out for their clients' welfare. They're going to address difficult questions and concerns up front. They take pride in what they do and how they do it. The really good ones often promise less, and deliver more.

Privacy Equals Value

As I stated earlier, the best way to improve the value of your home is to plant a tree. If there's one universal quality all potential homeowners are seeking - it's privacy. While you may love seeing your neighbors, most potential buyers would like to have outdoor living space that offers a feeling of privacy. That goes for looking out the window while in the home too. You may have a gorgeous home in a highly desirable neighborhood but if the feeling of privacy is heavily impacted by a neighboring property, it's almost always perceived as a negative when it comes to selling it. Oftentimes this is translated in the property selling for tens of thousands of dollars less than what might otherwise have been the case.

I'm constantly assessing and investigating properties. When I look at a subject and think, "Gee, if the seller had simply planted a tree or a few larger shrubs, the neighbor's view straight into the subject property would now be a non-issue", it's a real bummer. By strategically planting trees and shrubs you can create a tremendous amount of value for not a lot of money. You can buy a 5-gallon tree or large shrub for $35, plant it, and in three to four years, you can eliminate a huge issue that greatly impacts the feeling of privacy.

If those folks had done this, they likely would have added thousands or even tens of thousands of dollars to the value of their home. It can easily amount to as much as 5% of the total value of a property when it comes to eventually selling it. Even if the privacy issue doesn't bother you, it may bother a future owner, don't delay in addressing and mitigating this issue if it applies to you.

Getting Your Asking Price

No matter what we do to get your home sold, no matter how much money is spent on marketing, no matter how much effort is put into getting the home properly staged, there are two conditions that must be met prior to being able to effectively marketing a property. If these conditions are not met prior to receiving an offer - the sale will not be successful. First; the seller has to know where they're going when they sell their property. Transitioning out of their existing property into a replacement home is always going to be a key issue for sellers involved with the escrow process. If they have yet to secure a replacement property ready for them to move into at the closing - they absolutely must have a plan in place that realistically addresses the issue. Oftentimes I'll work with my clients for weeks or months to insure such a plan is in place prior to actively marketing their property. The Second condition is; the home has to be priced competitively against other competing properties in the marketplace. If these two things haven't happened or the conditions have yet to be met, most likely the home will not sell.

First and foremost, a Realtor® needs to know how take advantage of the marketplace. They need to know the inventory because there's usually a number of similarly priced competing properties available in a given marketplace. Often these properties will fit within the same search parameters as the subject property. Those other properties are either going to help you in the sale of your home or, you'll end up assisting those sellers in the sale of their property. Consumer sites now widely available on the Internet have really amplified this issue.

It's vitally important your Realtor® knows how to accurately determine what constitutes the marketplace for your property. The right Realtor® will be able to accurately show you how your property stacks up against these competing listings and how to use this information to your advantage. Competing properties might be limited to your own subdivision or they may be   located in three different cities.

Awareness of who your competition is or where it potentially lies can be a powerful tool when positioning your client for success in any market.   Possessing this kind of knowledge is essential when considering the behavior of the on-line buyer or seller.   This information can be utilized to position your client strategically in marketing and/or negotiations. Often it can result in significant gains for the client that potentially could be realized in negotiating leverage, favorable terms, or selling price. These advantages can be realized for both sellers and buyers.

Understanding how the power of the Internet can influence your marketplace is critically important when it comes to representing home sellers and buyers. Skilled experienced agents will know how consumer sites influence any given micro/macro marketplace. These sites tend to amplify whatever direction the prevailing winds are blowing. If inventory is building – buyers know it and they can get complacent.   If inventory is vanishing from the shelves rapidly – buyers often react with a greater sense of urgency. Knowing what's happening out there in cyberspace and how it's influencing your marketplace at any given time is essential. A good Realtor® will be able to address all these issues with you and perform accordingly.

The right Realtor® will often do multiple types of analysis when pricing their listings. When difficult questions need to be addressed - sometimes the answers revealed might not always be welcomed by sellers that have their own ideas. "How does the home stack up within your subdivision? How does it compete in the general neighborhood or community? In some cases we may also need to look at how we stack up in the greater North County area?" Agents oftentimes shy away from this. They may fail to do multiple types of analyses or they may only focus on a specific subdivision.   If the agent is not experienced or skilled in how to best compile and interpret this kind of data, it can sometimes put the client at a disadvantage, especially when it comes to harnessing the power and influence of our on-line marketplace.

Here's a perfect example. I recently listed a single level property on a golf course view lot. Single levels are rare in this particular area so there aren't many comps. Across the street, there was an exact model match that had been highly upgraded, however it was located on a corner lot with very little privacy in the backyard. You could literally drive by and look right into the kitchen windows through the backyard. That home had sold in the fall for $478,000. It went pending in 6 days about 4 months prior to the activation date of this new listing.

My seller had been told by another agent they'd interviewed that they would be able to get $510,000, maybe $515,000 max. While that agent had correctly adjusted for the view lot they may have failed to properly analyze how the subject property was stacking up in up in today's marketplace. While this home was indeed smaller than the other single level homes available in the area, there still wasn't anything available under $559,000. I ended up pricing that listing at $529,000. Within a week we had two full-price offers. To get the maximum price the market will bear the agent usually needs to do multiple types of analyses and be especially responsive to what the market is doing now rather than focusing solely on sales comps.

Overpricing a listing can be especially costly to a seller. If your listing is active in the on-line marketplace and it's priced beyond what the market will bear, you may have left the barn door wide open - creating plenty of room for competing neighboring properties to sell at a handsome price. What that overpriced seller really is doing, is helping that neighbor sell their home. Also, generally speaking, if you overprice your property, you'll find that the offers that are submitted (if you're lucky enough to get one) will not be coming in anywhere near your asking price. If you're $20,000 over market, you'll generally get an offer that's $40,000 below your asking price.

Most folks focus on pricing when interviewing a listing agent. "How much are you going to get me for my house?" What sellers and agents sometimes don't realize is - it's the market that will ultimately dictate the final figure - one way or another. What I try to do is put my clients in the very best position to harness and take full advantage of the marketplace that we find ourselves in right now. I'm always especially pleased when one or more neighboring sellers have overpriced their listings - leaving that barn door wide open.

More About the "NorthCountyHouseHunter"

I recently went back 15 years to track where my business came from. On an average annual basis 73% of my new business came from repeat and referred clients. I'm really quite proud of this because it tells me I truly must be doing some things right for my clients. This referral percentage is way above the industry average.

As far as awards go... In the 24 years I spent at Realty Executives I received multiple Diamond or Double Diamond awards. Each Diamond represented at least $10 million in sales. My first award was in 1999 and I went on to receive 12 more. In my first year (2014) I received the Bronze Award for production from my new company, Realty One Group in Carlsbad, CA.

In 2003 I received the Bronze Award from Realty Executives International. I had come in third out of 10,000 agents for production. That was the year I did 52 transactions, about $30 Million in sales as a solo agent (no team- no assistants). I was pretty busy that year. I didn't even know I'd won the award - they mailed it to me. No fanfare. I didn't mind because seeing the smiles on the faces of satisfied clients is the only award that really counts in this business.

Years ago I was present at Petco Park when the great San Diego Padre, Tony Gwynn, had his number retired. At that presentation Tony was asked: "As a Baseball Player - which of your talents or which qualities do you value most?" Tony's response: "Consistency." Every Padre fan on the planet knew that when you needed your best clutch player - you wanted Tony Gwynn – Tony was always the one you wanted at bat when the game was on the line.

I've always tried to work with my clients much as a consultant. Helping my clients build confidence in the process and educating my clients along the way is how I tend to operate. When it comes to helping my clients manage, what typically is their largest asset, it's important to treat them and their situation with the dignity and respect such an endeavor deserves. Consistency with this policy has been good for my clients and it's has been good for my business.

We've been married for 28 years. My wife Christine is a flight attendant for Delta Airlines. We raised our family here in North County and continue to support numerous community activities and group functions. We're big supporters of United Cerebral Palsy. UCP is really good at making sure the items and the monies donated get to the families that need it. When I have spare time I enjoy an occasional round of golf.

The Secret to Success

I list and sell residential Real Estate. My specialty is taking great care of my clients. It doesn't matter how much they're spending or what their home is selling for. It's about what my clients' specific needs are. It's extremely important to me that my clients have confidence in knowing I will always take excellent care of them - no matter what their situation is. People don't buy or sell homes very often. For most folks, their home remains the largest asset in their portfolio. So for me, it's very serious business.

I believe every family should have a trusted real estate agent, a Realtor® they can go to for consultation, referrals, and direction on the best ways to improve their property and preserve their asset. I tend to have that kind of relationship with my past clients. I often work with folks that have a desire to purchase or who are thinking of selling for months, even years, before they are ready to make a move or complete a transaction.

So much has changed about the Real Estate business over the last ten years – especially the speed at which it moves. Technology continues to change the way Real Estate is presented and marketed. To remain effective and take great care of my clients I've found I must continually develop new skills and stay educated on the most current up to date technology. It's the only way to effectively market Real Estate on a consistent basis.

Interestingly, little has changed about applying the skills necessary to successfully negotiate a sale or to navigate an escrow through to a successful closing. Sure, there is a ton more paperwork. There are new disclosure laws, reports, and multiple inspections, but when it comes to the client receiving the highest possible selling price and planning for an on time closing – these are the areas where experience really counts. It's really all about taking excellent care of the client and their family.

Listening, careful observation, asking the right questions - sometimes difficult ones, and constantly providing meaningful feedback to the client are perhaps the most important qualities a good Realtor® can possess. Consistently developing the art of listening with my clients while always keeping a close eye on, what ultimately, will be the best possible outcome for each and every one of those clients has really been the key ingredient involved with the success of my business. And I believe to the overall satisfaction of my clients.

Focusing on the larger aspect of what the best course of action may be for the client can sometimes result in the client making the decision NOT to purchase or NOT to sell at the present time. And that's always OK. It took a few years to get this - it was even a little scary at first - but once I learned to remove my own personal needs and desires from the equation, my business really started to grow. Remaining passionately focused on the needs and welfare of each and every client has truly been the secret to my success, and I believe, to a truly successful experience for all of my clients. For me it's what striving to become "the right" Realtor® is really all about. Perhaps this kind of passionate client focus can work for you as well.

Mark's Numbers

Total Transactions (Last 20 Years – 01/01/97 - 01/01/17) = 525

Listings Sold: (Seller Represented Transactions) = 312

Buyers Sold: (Buyer Represented Transactions) = 213

Average Sale to List Price Ratio – Listings Sold Last 20 Years = 98.63%

Average Market Time - Listings Sold Last 20 Years = 23 Days on Market

(Information compiled from Sandicor MLS: Transactions & Listings Sold from 01/01/97 – 01/01/17)

Legal: Total Number of Claims/Mediations/Arbitrations/Litigations = ZERO

10 Vital Questions to Ask a Realtor®
Before You Sign Anything!

You Deserve World Class Service
Learn How to Interview the Realtor®

1. How many years have you been in the real estate business? How many years have you been in the business here in North County?
2. How many different offices have you worked in? How long were you at each office? Why did you move?
3. How far back can you document your closed real estate transactions can you document in the Multiple Listing Service? What is that number? How many of these closed transactions were Listings - representing sellers? How many were buyer represented transactions?
4. What is the difference between a Realtor® and a Real Estate Agent? Are you a Realtor®?
5. Who will I be communicating with from the beginning and through to the end of the transaction? Will I be working with you exclusively or do you have a team? (If a team) How many others will I be communicating with? How often will I be communicating with them vs. you? Can you share their qualifications with me?
6. What are some of the things that can go wrong in a Real Estate Transaction? How do you prevent them from happening? What about the buyer's deposit?
7. Have you ever been involved in litigation surrounding one of your real estate transactions? If so - how many times? What were the issues involved and what was the result for your client(s)?
8. What percentage of your business is generated from referrals and repeat customers? Is this figure important to your business model? Why?
9. What is the average market time your listings sold over the last 5 years? What is your average sale to list price ratio for these listings?
10. Since buyers typically search the Internet for Listings, and since most Realtors® & agents show each other's Listings when posted in the MLS, why should I List my home with you instead a Discount Broker?

About the Author

Mark Hoadley

Realty ONE Group
Cal BRE Lic. # 01056402
2701 Loker Avenue West, Suite 150
Carlsbad, CA 92010

Phone: 760-525-5121
Mark@MarkHoadley.com
www.NorthCountyHouseHunter.com

Mark is a top producing Realtor® bringing 26 years of North San Diego County Real Estate experience to his office, Realty ONE Group, in Carlsbad CA. Mark operates chiefly as a full-time consultant when working with his clients throughout the home buying or selling process. Working one-on-one with his clients has always been important to Mark because of his constant concern for his client's welfare. Mark has avoided the team approach because he wants to ensure his clients are always making informed decisions. He has strong beliefs in the value of being able to personally keep his clients well informed and well educated throughout the home buying and home selling processes. Mark feels this approach also helps maintain continuity - which is vitally important when it comes to navigating a real estate transaction.

Perhaps it's this kind of care and concern Mark continues to demonstrate for his clients that made him the number one independent solo agent at his former office, Realty Executives, for 15 straight years (1998-2013). During that period 73% of Mark's sales volume was generated by repeat business and referrals from his past clients. That trend continues today. Mark credits his success to having consistently earned the trust of his customers. Mark says, "I remain truly grateful to my past clients - by sending referrals my way - they help my current clients because I'm no longer forced to spend valuable time promoting myself. Instead, I get to focus on what matters most: serving the needs of my clients."

34 Years in Real Estate and Still Sane

(although some may argue that point)

By Kathy Bartle

I was just starting college when my mother was diagnosed with terminal cancer. I put school on hold to help take care of her. During that time I was able to find a part-time job working for a title company. It was also during that time that my mother succumbed to cancer and passed away. She's been gone 34 years, but I still miss her every day.

While working for the title company I was introduced to a local Real Estate broker named Anne Coffman. She encouraged me to get my real estate license, hired me, and took me under her wing, teaching me everything she knew. I get a little emotional thinking about it still. Anne was not only my mentor; she was also my saving grace. I was devastated by the loss of my mother and had no direction. I don't know what she saw in me but whatever it was, I thank God and her everyday because she gave me my career.

Anne passed away in 2001 but I think of her often. My mother gave me my foundation; Anne gave me my future. I was so young when I started in real estate, I wondered if my age would be an issue. Anne never felt that way. Actually quite the opposite - she felt like it was an advantage. I was willing to work hard, put the time in, and do things the other more experienced Realtors® were not willing to do. It paid off.

I am property management certified and also a short sale and foreclosure resource. In addition, I am currently working on my senior real estate specialist certification that will allow me to assist the more mature market of 62 years and older, of which I am now fast approaching.

Hard Work Pays Off

When I first started out, I found my clients mainly by knocking on doors and holding open houses. Back then real estate offices also had what was called 'floor time' or 'floor duty'. That's when an agent is assigned a certain number of hours on certain days to be in the office and available to help any potential walk-in clients or telephone leads. None of us liked it, but when it paid off, it was worth it. There was no internet, so people would look through magazines or drive through neighborhoods they were interested in and see a "For Sale" sign. They would then call the office listed on the sign. Whoever was doing floor time during that period would get the lead. That is how I got most of my leads. I still keep in contact with many of those clients to this day and am now selling homes to their kids.

I also spend time doing what is called geographical farming. It's where you specialize in a certain neighborhood. For example, the neighborhood I 'farm' has 500 homes. I know all the floor plans, feeder schools, parks, and I know the people that live there. Everybody is interested in what the homes are selling for in their neighborhood. That's why, along with other marketing materials, I send out "Just Listed" and "Just Sold" flyers and I invite neighbors to my open houses.

The Communities I Represent

Although home base is in Fremont, CA, we also have offices in Livermore, Pleasanton, and San Jose. I work mainly in two counties: Alameda and Contra Costa. These counties consist of a total of approximately 20 cities.

Fremont is located between Silicon Valley and San Francisco. It's a highly desirable area for a number of reasons including its diverse population, central location and top ranking schools.

Fremont is the fourth largest city in California, and it is still growing with approximately 225,000 residents.

A few other reasons why Fremont is a Great Place to Live and Work

- Fremont has been voted one of "America's most inventive cities." (Newsweek, June 12, 2013)

- Fremont was voted No. 1 in the country for the number of startups per capita. (Sizeup.com, October 3, 2012)

- Fremont was ranked No. 2 best run city in the United States. (Wall Street 24/7, January 2, 2014)

- Fremont was ranked No. 3 on the Reader's Digest List of America's 10 Sharpest, Smartest Cities. (Readers Digest, October 14, 2012)

What I Love About Residential Real Estate

My specialty is residential real estate.

One of the things I pride myself on is that I am a good communicator. I communicate with my clients all the way through the escrow until closing and continue to keep in contact with them. I constantly remind myself that "This is their time... these two or three months that we're together is 100 percent their time" and give them the service they deserve. So anything they need, whether it's getting the house cleaned before they move in, meeting service people on their behalf, making hotel reservations for out of area buyers, arranging for a car, whatever they need... My team and I are happy to help.

Finding a buyer is only part of my job. I am also here to assist sellers by recommending improvements that will get them the biggest bang for their buck and the highest possible dollar value for their home. Here is the short list.

For sellers, my plan includes:

- Explain the step-by-step selling process
- Advertising (which includes professional photos and virtual tour)
- Promoting
- Negotiating the sale
- Handling the Appraisal
- Organizing Inspections
- My team and I also provide bids on work with trusted tradesmen that might be needed.
- Accompanying you to the closing

...And of course, assuring you receive your proceeds immediately.

Buyers can expect:

- An accurate estimate of the total cash required to purchase your home
- To be shown homes available regardless of which real estate company has it listed or advertised
- To be signed up for my "auto-notification" program notifying you immediately of new listings so you will never miss an opportunity
- A step by step explanation of the purchasing process
- To be guided through that process once you have found your home
- Negotiation for the best possible deal for you
- To be provided bids on work with trusted tradesmen that might be needed

...And it will be my pleasure to deliver the keys to you at close.

Location, Location, Location . . . it really is true!

When buying a home, it is all about location. I cannot stress that enough. Everything about a home can be altered. You can change the walls, the floor plan, the size of the house, the color, but you cannot change the location. This is also important to keep in mind for resale purposes. My number one piece of advice for buying a home is: You must buy in a good location, especially if you are expecting to make money on the resale.

When clients are moving to the Bay Area from a different city or from out of state, they don't always know the area. That's where I come in. I was born and raised here so I know everything there is to know about the area. I know all the neighborhoods, the schools, and where the nearest grocery store is. I can tell potential buyers what to expect as far as appreciation rate in a neighborhood and the demographic make-up such whether it has mostly older and established people, young professionals or are they mostly young families that live in the area. I also know the best hiking trails and restaurants. I can provide the buyer with other referrals such as dentist, doctor, dry cleaner, and other professional services they may need.

For condo and townhouse buyers, there are some things they need to know ahead of time to get the best resale value. One of the more obvious considerations is to make sure there is no litigation or lawsuits against the complex. Lenders won't lend and it has a negative effect on property value. Other things to consider would be if the unit has inside laundry. Does the unit have direct access to an attached garage? Does the complex have ample guest parking? You don't want your guests to have to hike into the complex to get to your place. Once again, location is absolutely crucial.

What to keep in mind when buying a home

When buying a home, you want to keep in mind that the average person lives there for only 5-7 years.

Here are some things to consider:

- If you don't already have children, are you planning on it?

- If you are thinking of having children, will the floor plan work? Some people would prefer 2 stories while others may prefer single levels.

- Are you comfortable with the school attendance area of the neighborhood? A bit of caution: because of the overcrowding of many schools, your child may be bused to a less crowded school regardless of the attendance area. If this is a concern, check with the school district ahead of time.

- It's not unusual to have multi-generational families moving in together. Is there enough space for Mom and Dad? Will they have areas in the house they can call their own?

- Does the home fit your lifestyle? What about your commute?

I recently listed a townhouse for sale that I had previously sold to the client 14 years earlier, before they had children. Since then, their family has grown. They now have four children in a townhouse that they had converted into a three bedrooms. Although they did a beautiful job with the conversion, it still didn't fit the needs with their growing family. Together, we sold that townhouse and they purchased a home within a mile from their old home that was big enough to fit all of their family needs.

Financing

Financing is the foundation of the purchase. Because of the complexities, you need to partner with a lender who will help you navigate through the maze of paperwork. You need to choose someone you know and trust, not the online lender that promises you the world. If you do not know anyone, then would I encourage you to ask around for a referral from a friend or a relative who has had a good experience. If that does not work, I am happy to refer my clients to a couple of priority lenders that I've had excellent experiences with over the years.

Selling Your Home

The first and most important factor of selling your home is to price it competitively. It has to be priced correctly right from the get-go. Don't try to 'test' the market by overpricing your home. That never works and almost always ends up getting a lower price than you deserve because of the length of time it stays on the market. A listing gets stale when on the market too long. Remember: the faster the sale, the more likely you're going to get your price. The first offer is usually the best offer.

The second most important factor is curb appeal. When a buyer pulls up to a home, they are already making a judgment call. Therefore, it is imperative that the front of the home is in good repair. If it needs paint, then paint. If the landscaping needs to be spruced up, do that. You may need to plant some flowers. Replace address numbers if needed and don't forget to sweep away any cobwebs. Take a good, hard look at the front of the home garage door all the way down to the mailbox.

Another very important thing to do is de-clutter. We tend to over-accumulate possessions when we live in a home for many years. It is of the utmost importance that you de-clutter and deep clean your home prior to selling it so it creates the least amount of distractions as possible when people are viewing. So that means no knickknacks or anything that can take the buyer's focus away from the house. We want them to look at the house, not at your stuff. In this case, less is more.

If your house is empty, it's important to get it staged. This is especially crucial in the San Francisco Bay Area. If it is done right, you will likely sell the home for more money and quicker than if you didn't stage. Staging is not cheap, but if you have the right stager, it is well worth the cost.

Perseverance

Sometimes a sale can go south pretty quickly. I remember one from 1992 which actually won me the Going the Extra Mile award. These clients became friends for life, and they have since sold and purchased many homes through me over the years.

With that transaction, I represented Ron and Mia, a young newly married couple expecting their first child. They were first time home buyers who had been renting an apartment. We searched and searched and we finally found the one! It was vacant, met all their criteria perfectly, and was within their price range. We made the offer and the seller accepted. My clients gave notice on their apartment and we continued to move through the escrow process. Unbeknownst to us or the seller, it was discovered during escrow that there were a number of liens on the house, none of which had any dollar amounts. After further research we found that the liens exceeded the owner's equity. This meant that the escrow may not close and therefore, Ron and Mia would not be able to move into the home. To complicate matters, they only had a matter of days to move out of their apartment and Mia was ready to give birth any day.

I negotiated with the seller to see if we could let the buyers rent the house until we could find them another home or another place to rent. The seller agreed.

We negotiated the rent for $900 a month. While Mia was in the hospital giving birth to their first child, Ron got everything moved into the house. The hospital kept Mia an extra day while Ron organized the furniture and set up the crib. It was just crazy.

If that wasn't enough, the seller's lender started foreclosure proceedings against the seller. The foreclosure process went through as my clients were living there. This meant that the lender could potentially evict Ron and Mia. We were stunned and not really sure what to do. I decided to go the lender and plead our case, "You've got a buyer that loves the house and has the money to buy it. They've already been preapproved for their loan. Rather than having to evict them and go through long arduous process, please consider their offer to buy the home". We presented the offer to the lender - they accepted! We finalized the sale shortly thereafter. Whew, potential crisis averted.

The unexpected bonus at the end of this whole fiasco was that even though we negotiated a rent of $900 a month and they were living there from August to November, during that time the seller skipped town and could not be found. The rent was never paid to anyone because nobody could ever find the seller. Ron and Mia lived there rent-free for 4 months.

It was a very trying time. Luckily, my clients trusted me enough to allow me to navigate our way through such an unusual situation. In the end, everything worked out; the buyers got their home! The day that Ron went to pick up Mia and the baby from the hospital, I went over to the house with balloons and put a big banner on the garage that said, "It's a girl!" My hope was when they rounded the corner it would help put a smile on Mia's face. What a time it was. To this day, we are still friends. Since then, I have helped them sell and purchase other homes.

There was another time that my perseverance paid off in a situation that ended up being kind of funny. I was showing a vacant home to a first time homebuyer, Chris. It was my first time meeting her but we had a lot in common. I pulled up to the first house on the list of homes we were going to see that day. It was a two story with a nice curb appeal. Since it was vacant, I used the lockbox to let us in. We viewed the interior first, and then went from the kitchen through the garage, and into the backyard. When we finished admiring the professionally landscaped and very private backyard, we headed toward the patio door to back inside but it was locked. No problem. We'll just go back the way we came, through the side garage door. Uh oh, that door was locked too. It must have locked when it closed behind us. We're now stuck in the backyard of a vacant house with my keys and my phone locked inside the house!

Chris suggested we go through the gate at the front of the house. It was padlocked! I told Chris, "You're going to have to go over the fence", to which she replied, "Hell no! I'm not going over that fence!" Fine. So I shimmied over the fence - high heels and all. I finally got over, let myself in through the front door that was still unlocked, and got in the house. It was all very professional, you know. We became good friends and still laugh about that debacle. She's bought and sold many homes with me over the years.

How I Feel About Holding Open Houses

I do hold open houses. Most sellers would prefer not to have an open house as it's an uneasy feeling having so many strangers walk through your home, not always accompanied by an agent. Most sellers assume they have to have hold their home open as part of the selling process. Open houses are just one of the many marketing tools we discuss at the listing appointment. They are great for the listing agent because that's how we get our clients. Neighbors coming through are potential sellers and people coming through are potential buyers. However, one of the misconceptions is that sellers feel like an open house will sell their home. Sometimes it does, but most times the people that attend open houses are not always ready, willing and more importantly, able buyers. Serious buyers will have an agent and the agent will show the house regardless if it's held open or not. When push comes to shove, it's the seller decision to make.

Preparing Your Home for Sale

Paint, paint, and paint some more. It changes the whole ambiance of a home. The next question becomes, "What color?" Stay with neutral colors. You have to appeal to the masses, and neutral colors do this. The more specific your style, the less people you're going to attract. So keep it neutral. This should go without saying but if you have the old acoustic or popcorn ceilings texture that so popular in the 1950's to the 1980's, scrape it off, texture and paint it. It'll change your world.

New carpeting is always a great improvement. If it needs to be changed out, again, do a neutral color. New baseboards and crown molding are equally cost effective enhancements. If you have hardwood flooring, it may be a good time to have it refinished. Another great improvement would be to change out older flat panel interior doors with six panel doors or something similar. It really updates the house.

Often a seller will opt to give the buyer a monetary credit to be redeemed at the close of escrow rather than do the repairs or improvements themselves. In theory, that does sound reasonable, but the reality is that most buyers cannot visualize the potential improvements. They will either decline the credit and want the work completed before they move in or they will ask for a disproportionate amount of money to do the work after they move in. In the long run, it is often more cost-effective for the seller to just make the improvements.

When I go on a listing appointment, I already have an idea of who the buyer will be. Because I have been in the business as long as I have and I know the neighborhoods and have done extensive research, I know what buyers are looking for. For example, I know that in one particular neighborhood, it is likely that the buyer will be a young professional couple that makes good money and probably works in the tech field, maybe Silicon Valley. People like that are not terribly interested in big backyards and doing a lot of yard maintenance. They are going to want to be able to buy a home that will not require much work and basically they can just move right in. If I am in a neighborhood like that, I will advise the sellers to do different improvements than I would in a neighborhood that is more geared for family and younger children.

The improvements a home may need really depends on neighborhood and the house itself. The goal here is to get the seller the biggest bang for their buck. As Realtors®, we can suggest improvements that better the odds of them getting their monies worth and more. For example, if a kitchen needs to be remodeled or needs cabinets, it might be better to just paint the cabinets and change out the hardware rather than replace them. Sometimes, a full remodel may be necessary. Kitchens and baths sell homes, so that is where you will find most of my recommendations.

Why You Should Use a Local Realtor®

I own investment properties outside my service area. Even though I am a real estate broker, I still use the area's local Realtors®. They know the local laws and the neighborhoods. There are many people involved in an escrow and many regulations. It takes an average of 30 people to make a transaction come together and over 150 emails and phone calls to coordinate a successful close. And even with all that, you are still likely going to have some sort of hiccup. So if you do not know how, or do not have the experience, you will not have the intuitiveness to know what may happen. If seller tries to sell on their own, the likelihood is that they will probably lose money because they are not marketing to the right people. A buyer may end up paying more because they do not have the knowledge that a local agent would be able to provide.

It is important to hire someone who knows the neighborhoods and knows the area. There could be a situation where maybe four doors down from the house that the client is interested in has a sinkhole or the fault line runs through their neighborhood. A local

Realtor® would know that and disclose it to the buyer. Many homeowners do not understand that if the seller is aware of something like that, they must disclose that information, it's the law. That could determine whether a buyer would want to buy in that neighborhood or not.

For example, in our area, there are some pockets that are flood zone areas where Flood insurance is mandatory. It's not cheap. If you're the buyer you're going to want to know that fun fact from the get-go.

If you are selling locally, hire locally. Local agents know the local market. Ask them how familiar they are with your neighborhood.

- How many homes have they sold in your neighborhood?

- Do they know the schools? Most buyers will buy homes in good school attendance areas.

- Do they know the API (Academic Performance index) scores of the local school? Buyers will ask. Your agent will need to know.

- How far is shopping?

- The library?

- Other amenities?

Do yourself a favor and hire an experienced, local agent who knows the neighborhood.

Realtors'® Responsibilities

The number one complaint we hear from buyers and sellers is lack of communication with their agent. The agent picks up the listing, and then they do not communicate with the seller again unless, or until, there is an offer to present. It is crucial to communicate with the seller during the listing process. When the time comes where negotiating is in play, the seller and the Realtor® have to be on the same page. Same goes for the buyer. They need reassurance through the process, even if it's nothing new to report. A phone call or an email every few days goes a long way.

An honest, down to earth conversation with your client is always best. It may not always be pleasant, but it will always be best. My goal as a real estate broker is to get the seller highest price and the buyer the best deal. The only way to do that is keeping an open, honest line of communication throughout the entire process. It makes for a much smoother transaction and a win-win for both sides.

To help facilitate a smooth, quick sale I recommend two things.

1. Get all your inspections done ahead of time. Do it before you put the house on the market and provide them to the buyer before they make their offer.   The three most common include a Pest inspection, a Roof inspection and a Home inspection. Your Realtor® will advise which ones should seriously be considered and there may be others such as a Chimney inspection, sewer inspection, pool inspection, etc.

2. Have all the required sellers' disclosures fully completed and available to the buyer before he makes his offer. This serves two purposes. For the seller, it gives them a heads-up on what repairs a buyer may request and also allows them to leverage their negotiating knowing what repairs may be needed. For a buyer, it gives them a very good idea on the condition of the house which allows them to make an educated, less emotional decision should they decide to make an offer.

A Most Rewarding Career

After 34 years in the real estate business, I can truly say that I am so grateful to my mentor, Anne Coffman, for encouraging me to take a leap of faith and study for my real estate license. She guided me and taught me everything I needed to know. I am so glad I took the chance and listened to her. One of the most gratifying aspects of my business is that I now get to help the children of my past clients. Some were not even born when I sold their parents their first home and now, these children buying their first homes. I love it! I have thoroughly enjoyed

– and continue to enjoy – my career to this day. Nothing makes me happier than to connect the right people to the right properties and find them their perfect homes.

About the Author

Kathy Bartle

Kathy Bartle
Legacy Real Estate & Associates
41111 Mission Blvd, Fremont, CA. 94539.
Offices also in Pleasanton, Livermore and San Jose

Office Phone: 510.743.1981
Mobile Phone: 510.589.3509
Email: Kathybartle@comcast.net
www.BartleRealtyGroup.com

Facebook Business Page: https://www.facebook.com/pages/Kathy-Bartle-Broker-Associate-Legacy-Real-Estate/208000142547462
Twitter: @KathyBartle
LinkedIn: Linkedin.com/in/bartlerealtygroup

Kathy Bartle was born and raised in the San Francisco Bay area. She has been selling real estate full time since 1981 and received her Brokers license in 2001.

She is a former real estate manager and real estate trainer. In 2015, this will be her 34th year practicing Real Estate. After managing a real estate office, Kathy went back into working one-on-one with clients, as she felt that her talents were more valuable and it was much more rewarding interacting with clients.

Kathy has been awarded the following Honors

- Centurion Award Recipient

- Winners Circle Award Recipient

- Bay East Association of REALTORS® President Club, Masters Club and Grand Masters Club

- Top Producer 30 consecutive years
- Leader's Circle of Success
- Circle of Achievement Award Recipient
- Going the Extra Mile Award Recipient

Kathy has 3 children. Her son, Ryan, is 25 and her twin daughters Kori and Casey are 23. They all are independent and have careers of their own.

My Journey to a Career in Real Estate

By Rudy LaBrada

As a kid, I was always fascinated with designing homes. I used to sit on my front porch and draw floor plans and pictures of houses and once built a house using balsa wood from a floorplan I had collected at a new home development. However, real estate was not the career path I took in college at Loyola Marymount University.

In my political science classes, the professor thought I had potential, so he sent me on an interview for a job as an intern for a member of the Assembly who was running for state office. They had already filled the job by the time I was referred, but luckily for me, they unfilled it and hired me. This started my career in politics.

I did some amazing things in politics, but at the age of 26, in 1991, after working on a grueling gubernatorial race, I decided it was time for a change. I obtained my real estate license and initially went to work for my sister and brother-in-law, who were also in real estate, but along the way I met a friend who was a broker named Debbie Iketani. She became my mentor and I began to work for her. She was not a power broker by any means, but she knew the legalities, the

97

contracts, the ins and outs, what to do, how to respond, how to react, and those were the components of the real estate business I pulled from her that created my foundation. I worked with her for several years before I started The LaBrada Group in 1997.

Our office is in downtown Upland, which is basically a small historic village neighborhood. This area is called the Inland Empire, and we are about 45 minutes outside of Los Angeles on the east side of town. This is a fairly sizeable bedroom community on the outskirts of Los Angeles.

Jobs are plentiful here. We have a very vast job market here. We have a large airport, Ontario International Airport, which is a very good place to work. We also have several trucking hubs nearby. Amazon.com just opened up a warehouse out in San Bernardino which is about 20 minutes or so away. Surprisingly though, I have a huge clientele of teachers and people in law enforcement.

Why I Love Real Estate

I think the best part about real estate is that you wake up every morning and do not know what your day is going to be like.

Your day could be very calm, and everything could go right. Or, it could just be a day of problem-solving and everything in-between. The other upside is you are not always in the office; you are out showing properties, meeting with clients, attending inspections, overseeing rehabs and repairs etc. There is a social component to being in real estate too. Every day is different, and that is the part I like. Being cooped up in an office all day just does not work for me.

Being an independent is difficult because I am not only a real estate broker, I am also a small business owner. So, I worry about things like payroll, taxes, municipal issues, running a small office and all the things that go along with running a business.

Also, when you own the business and it is your name on the door, and, with that I believe, there is a higher realm of ethics and pride because, ultimately, it is your name on the line. When I shake a person's hand and I look in their eyes, they know that I am going to do what I say I will do. It goes back to old world ethics and the time spent with my maternal grandfather, John LaBrada, a great man who taught me many things through his own actions.

I specialize in single family homes and property management. My sister runs my property management division. About a year after hiring her, I also hired my niece, who does all of my social media. In today's world, I have found that social media is increasingly more important as a way of staying connected and attracting new clients, in particular millennials. We need to stay connected using our updated website, integration of new social media platforms, a monthly newsletter, property tour videos and more, with this, we are generating a new type of buzz for the company.

I have always been an independent agent and always with a small office, so accolades have never really been my source for motivation. However, somehow I was awarded one of the top 250 Latino real estate agents in America. I have no idea how I got nominated for that, but was happy non-the-less to make the list!

Inherent Vulnerabilities in Business

I think you always feel vulnerable in this industry. There is no way around it; no matter how confident I am, I will always have vulnerability on several levels. Every time you pick up the phone or meet a new client, you have to sell yourself. Not taking things personally is a very difficult thing to maneuver through for anybody. You also feel vulnerable because of the kind of world we live in; meeting new clients for the first time, or showing a vacant property and worrying about your safety and the safety of my staff.

The last economic downturn was a lesson in many things, in particular, stamina, accounting and creativity. The fact that I majored in business in college helped as did the fact my mother was a small business owner until she retired about five or six years ago, so combining book smarts, street smarts and a lot of luck, I was able to keep our doors open. During this last downturn, I think at one point there were about 20 or more real estate offices in this little downtown area, and it literally went down to one. I have been in this office for 14 plus years. I persevered and I made the cuts I needed to make in order to survive, and I survived.

Important Factors When Buying a Home

Instead of stating the usual "location, location, location" I always start off my asking my clients, "Do you see your family living here?" And if the answer is yes and if your gut is telling you that this is it, then this is it. So, first and foremost, listen to yourself, do not listen to what some salesperson is telling you – listen to what your gut reaction is in the first three steps of walking in that house or as you pull up in the driveway.

So to me, gut reaction is number one. Then number two would be location. After that, if you have children, you'll need to think about the school district and proximity to schools. Listen to yourself and then listen to all the other factors that directly impact you.

I am very into Feng Shui and will have my sellers on my listings, for instance, do certain things such as specific object placement. I tell them the basic things like 'keep the toilet lid down, think positive thoughts, dispense with negativity.' If they have bad energy in a certain place in their house, unpopped popcorn in a glass jar under the toilet is a good way to absorb the bad energy. Crystals, moving furniture around, those are all things I suggest to people. Sometimes, I tell them it is Feng Shui, but if I do not sense they would be open to that concept, I just say, "Indulge me and let me do a couple of things to your house."

I tend to be very opinionated which is why they like me because I will say, "No, I am not going to show you that house, and these are the reasons why." Or, we will walk into a house, and I will say, "No, this is not the house for you, and these are the reasons why."

I like to get to know my clients well enough so I know what they need even if they do not know what they need. I try to do what I call a needs-wants assessment with each new client. Not all clients are willing to do this though; people do not want to talk to you on the phone, they do not want to come in for a face-to-face, they want to do everything on the internet and emails. Then, you start showing them houses and you have to pull the information out of them. I prefer to do a needs-wants interview here in the office where I basically get to know them. Who are you? What do you do? How did you meet? Tell me about your kids. Where do you go to church? How far away do you work? Do you have lots of family parties? Those type of questions. Then I give them the honest truth. If I ask, "Tell me what you are looking for," and they say they want a mansion, I will say, "Well, you can't afford a mansion, but how about a one bedroom condo?" Of course, that is the extreme, but sometimes I have to give them a reality check.

This is also a good way for me to get to know them but, more importantly, for them to get to know me. I think it helps that I am the owner of this business and it is my name on the door, that I have been in the business for 24 years, and that I was probably referred to them by someone they respect. All of those things create the loyalty you do not see very often in this industry.

Financing Issues

I give advice about financing all the time. In fact, I have clients right now who I have represented three times on different things they have done. So they know me. They trust me. He is a police officer, she works in a school. They said, "We need to figure out what we're doing. We're not really sure." So I basically put a plan together for them. Sometimes they just need someone to help them figure out what path to take.

When my clients are young, I tell them the things I wish someone had told me. Like save your money. Do not waste your money. Do not go buy crazy cars. I do not want to drive by here and see a new car parked in your driveway. Save for your retirement. Trust me. I am turning 50. You are 25. It literally comes around the corner very quickly. Things like that.

I am also not a fan of selling houses even though I am in the sales industry. I think that if you can keep your house and buy a new house some other way, do it that way because you only create wealth for the most part by using someone else's money. I break it down very simply. Here is the reality, if you have a $200,000 asset, and the market goes up by 10 percent, you make $20,000. If you have $20,000 in the bank and the market goes up and you have it at 2 percent, you make $400. It is very simple. You just have to figure out how to do it. Sometimes, you have to make the sacrifices to do it. I learned this lesson late in my career and wish I had learned it earlier.

I have clients who own multiple houses which is why I started my property management company. Initially, I had to teach my assistant how to manage my own properties. As I got older, my business got older and my clients would come to me and say, "We think we want to diversify. We think we want to do something. We have this money sitting here." And so I would say, "Okay. Let's go buy this house. And I will manage it for you."

The reason people come back to me is because they know that if they call me, they are not going to get pressured and they will get the truth. My philosophy is to create clients over the long-term, it is not about the short-term. If we go back to why I survived the downturn, it is because people came back to me because they knew I would give them the truth. If you are good to people, they are good back to you. You tell them the truth, they appreciate you. They never forget you.

Saving Deals

The day before yesterday, I had a deal fall out of escrow. I was explaining to my seller, that in the world of offers and real estate, that was one buyer who I would never have thought would fall out of escrow. She had the money in the bank, she had the job, and I had even talked with her lender, and she had 7 something FICO score, a nice high score. Who is going to think that her ex-husband is going to file bankruptcy with her debts a week into the escrow? Nobody! You just do not ever think that. There are certain things that do not come into your head until it happens. In this case, it did not work out for her, but here's what I did: I went back to the people who made a back up offer on the property and said, "Do you still want it?" and they said, "Yes!" And so we are reopening escrow today on that deal.

I do what I can to save the deal. For my sellers, it is a couple of thousand dollars less, but the close date is basically the same. Ultimately, it is all going to work out. And that is the lesson: Everything happens for a reason. As you go down the path, oftentimes it becomes clearer why it happened.

Showing Homes

In all of my years in real estate, I have had funny, dramatic, and traumatic experiences showing homes.

Very early in my career, I had planned an Open House for a listing when the sellers were going to be out of town that weekend. I noticed they had some big, beautiful plants in the backyard beside the pool. At first, I thought they were tomato plants, but upon closer inspection I realized they were marijuana plants! I talked to the sellers and said, "You have to get rid of those plants. I am having an open House this weekend." They said, "Ok, we'll put them away." I was worried about it but they assured me everything would be ok. When I got to the open house with my associate, the first thing I did was look for the plants. The only thing they did was wrap big black trash bags around them! They were so big – it looked completely ridiculous.

Looking out the window, you could see trash bags all around these five or six huge, six or eight foot plants. What could I do? I did the open house. People were coming. Nobody said anything. Then, the wind starts. My associate and I are literally running out in the backyard, fixing the bags, letting people through, running back out to the yard, fixing again and timing when they go in the backyard. It was crazy and exhausting! Ultimately, I sold the house that day.

The most painful and tramatic experience was with a domestic violence incident. I had a townhouse listed and I was having quite a hard time selling this townhouse. I felt fortunate that I had a couple come back for a third showing. I was doing my very best to show them the house again. We were at the top of the stairs when suddenly all hell breaks loose. We heard screaming and a door slam. Then, a naked lady runs right past the living room! She was screaming and bleeding. Her husband had cut half her hair off and he was screaming and hollering behind the locked door to let him in. I ran downstairs, and yelled at the wife that was looking at the house to find something to cover this poor woman. Then I yelled at her husband to call 911. And I used every ounce of my being to keep the door locked.

Once the police arrived and we knew she was safe, we were asked to leave. The buyers left, never to return. And there I was, still selling this damn unit. I had to see the lady and her husband fairly often. It seemed like they were outside whenever I went to the unit. They never mentioned the incident. In fact, they did not even say, "Hi." Eventually, I sold the unit, and that was the end of it.

You just never know what you are going to find. You make your appointments, you tell people you are coming, and you never know how people are going to react or what you are going to find when you open up a front door. Even after all these 24 years in this industry, it always makes me a little nervous to open the door and say, "Real estate. I am here to show your house."

The Internet is the Best Marketing Tool

The only print advertising I do are color brochures. Virtually, all of my marketing is done on the internet. Clients can go to my website, the MLS and to sites like Zillow and Trulia. In addition, each listing is disseminated to a variety of websites and social media such as Facebook, Instagram and our YouTube channel. Research shows at least 90 percent of all home buyers start to search on the internet so it's crucial that we make our pictures and descriptions as appealing as possible.

I also do home staging on every listing. I do everything from a partial stage to a full stage. I go through the house with a homeowner and say, "Remove this. Do this. Do that. Let's move that picture here and let's get a mirror here. Let's do this. Let's put a whole bowl of fruit here to pull the eye that way. And when you walk in this room, this is where the eye goes. And that is really not where it needs to go." So that is a partial stage when it is occupied. I will also bring in accessories to the kitchens, the bathrooms, over the fireplaces, things to pull the eye in different directions to elongate rooms or move the eye to where you want them to focus and to basically make the house have some sort of warmness versus being some empty, vacant house.

We have all the staging pieces here in the office. I also have a room at home filled with pictures and plants of all kinds. I tell people when I am on listing appointments, "Did you go through my listings on my website when you looked at the vacant properties? You will see all the staging pieces for the most part." I offer to stage the property for free because I have all the pieces and it adds value to my service. In fact, my sister does the staging for me. People love it, it is part of the process, and it helps sell more quickly.

To get the maximum asking price for the home you really need to do the staging. There are various degrees to the staging as I explained. If a house is torn up and ugly, there is not a whole lot you can do to it, but if the seller is willing to make some repairs, it helps. Sometimes, just a deep cleaning, dust the window sills, dust your window coverings, and have someone come in and clean your windows will make a big difference, even on a fixer upper. Just the basics to get the smell and energy right.

Real Estate Agent 101

When hiring a real estate agent to assist you in your home sale or purchase, you need to know what kind of experience they have. How many years have they been in the business? Are they a broker or an agent? Are they full-time or part-time? How many homes a year do they sell? I am a firm believer that if you want something done right, you give it to a busy person to do. Also ask if they have ever been sued. But, most people will not answer that question correctly or honestly. It goes back to intuition, that gut feeling. Are you feeling this person is going to do right by you? If the answer is yes, then go with them, but also be loyal. I am a big fan of loyalty.

When people call and say, "I have been working with an agent, but I want to switch," I will say, "Well, what is that agent not doing for you?" And they will say, "Oh, they just haven't found my house." "Well, are they showing you houses or are they taking you to houses?" And literally, I will talk people into keeping their agent. If, ultimately, you decide you want to switch, call me. I am happy to help you, but give the guy a chance, the market is tough right now. Or, I tell them that they need to make themselves available more frequently to go look at houses because they are selling so quickly.

From the selling side the process is pretty straight forward. I go on the listing appointment. I do my listing presentation. They either sign the paperwork there or they call me back later after they interview other agents or whatever and say, "Okay. We're ready." I have them sign the papers. Once they sign the papers, we start getting the home ready for sale.

Once they have signed the listing agreement, I go back in and do the staging part. Every house I list gets something. Some owners are more open to doing things than others; for the most part you will not ever see me have a dirty listing. Even if it is a tear-down, it will still get cleaned. I send in cleaners and if the owner will not pay for it, I will.

I then either have the house shot by a professional photographer or I do the photography myself. Either way, I am there. Once the pictures are ready, we upload them onto the MLS and all the different websites and social media platforms. We also have a flyer prepared which I design myself. Then the sign goes up. We then schedule an open house if they want it. Internet marketing gets started, and then we continually do something to get the word out that this home is available.

Then the showings start. Once offers come in, you prepare the net sheet. You look at the offer and make sure that the i's are dotted and the t's are crossed. I meet with the homeowner to review the offers, giving them the pros and cons of each offer (assuming there are multiple offers), and then selecting the one that works best.

Some of the factors of a good offer are: the lender, their agent's reputation or lack of reputation in town, and how the offer is written - some agents do not have the training or knowledge to properly write an offer - and finally, FICO scores, proof of funds, and the basic buyer qualifications.

It is not just about the number and it is not just about who the buyer is. It is about a whole series of things. You need to look at all of those factors before you can evaluate which offer is best.

When you work with me, or any real estate agent, you can expect results, timely responses, honesty, ethics, and knowledge. People use all sources to contact me; text, call, email. I am a classic type A personality. I am, for the most part, always available. I do not like to fly, so I have a motor home. So, when I go on vacation, I have my computer, printer, scanner, and fax machine. Sometimes, my clients do not even know I am on vacation because things move along status quo.

I believe my clients choose me over other real estate agents because they get all that I have described, and I really do take the time to get to know them and let them know they are in good hands. Plus, the vast majority of my clients are referred to me. When they come to me from a referral source, you start with an initial bond, which creates loyalty. Then, everything else kicks in and they know you will take care of them.

The most rewarding thing about this job is that every day is different. I also love that I have generations of families as clients. It is amazing that I am now selling homes to the children of my clients! It is nice to see these individuals grow up and watch their careers and families bloom.

About the Author

Rudy LaBrada

The LaBrada Group
BRE #01117345
155 East "C" Street, Suite D
Upland, CA 91786

Tel: 909-981-3500
Fax: 909-981-3462
http://www.thelabradagroup.com
Rudy.LaBrada@gmail.com

Rudy LaBrada has been in real estate for more than 23 years. In 1997 Rudy opened his first Downtown Upland office later moving his location down the street and has been here ever since. Rudy attended Bishop Amat Memorial High School and received his Bachelor's in Business Administration from Loyola Marymount University. In addition to being a licensed Real Estate Broker, Rudy is a Certified Short Sale and Foreclosure Specialist.

Most people would be interested to know that Rudy has a background in political finance. Previously, Rudy was a Finance Director for politicians for statewide and national office. He worked with individuals that were, and continue to be, very prominent politicians on the state and national level. Politics was a great career path when he was younger but later became more difficult when not allowing for family time. When looking for his second career he knew that real estate was his passion.

Rudy would describe himself as loyal, trustworthy, and silly. In his spare time he enjoys tending to his beautiful garden, taking trips in his motor home, relaxing on the beach, and playing with his two dogs, Molly and Buddy.   You can follow Rudy on Facebook by liking The LaBrada Group.

Real Estate Found Me

By Stacy Young

Real estate actually found me. My dream was to become an opera singer. Having trained locally and in Europe, I had a plan in place. When I graduated college in 1975, my mother's best friend, a local Realtor® with Coldwell Banker, helped me get a summer job as an administrative assistant at the top Westside real estate office.

At the end of the summer, they no longer needed my services and I found a position with another real estate company, Philip Norton, Inc., because I had enjoyed the summer job so much. Eventually, Coldwell Banker called me and said, "Our office manager position is available and we'd love for you to come back." I returned to that office and worked my way up the corporate ladder. It just seemed to be a good match and with that, I launched my career in real estate.

I continued to pursue my musical career, but I found I liked real estate and it paid far more. Meeting new people, expanding my knowledge of the business world and embracing new challenges all appealed to me. Tim Corliss recruited me to join his company, Corliss & Associates with 13 offices on the Westside of Los Angeles including the San Fernando Valley. I was hired as the Operations Manager, responsible for opening and closing offices, and for all of their personnel. I then moved into marketing and public relations and taught some training classes for new Realtor® Associates. But the market was changing and so was the face of Westside real estate.

After a few years away from real estate to start a family, enjoying Santa Barbara and north county San Diego along the way, I returned to Los Angeles to find Merrill Lynch had bought Corliss & Associates, and Merrill Lynch Realty was born. I was asked to head the marketing department for all 17 offices, continuing to work my way up the corporate ladder to Senior Vice President. People kept asking me, "Why don't you get your real estate license?" I would think, "I couldn't sell my way out of a paper bag." Finally, in 1992 I decided to get my license. I started selling real estate and found I truly loved it. Helping buyers realize their dreams of homeownership and assisting sellers with the next phase of their lives was a natural for me. So real estate just found me!

My Philosophy on Selling

I don't see the process of selling real estate as sales. Someone has already made the decision to either sell or buy real estate and I'm the facilitator. I help guide my clients through the process. It's a very complicated process, especially if you've never gone through it before. With over 23 years of experience behind me, the process has become very fluid for me. It's very rewarding helping clients with one the largest investments in their lives.

Where I Work

The primary geographic location of my business is the Westside of Los Angeles. This encompasses a large area including Bel Air, Brentwood, Beverlywood, Beverly Center/Miracle Mile, Century City/Westwood, Culver City, Palms/Mar Vista, Mid-Wilshire, Marina del Rey, Playa Vista, Playa Del Rey, Pacific Palisades, Santa Monica, Venice, and Westchester. I've also represented clients in the South Bay that encompasses Manhattan Beach, Redondo Beach and Hermosa Beach and to the north in the San Fernando Valley areas of Sherman Oaks, Encino, Studio City and Tarzana.

Each market performs a little bit differently. I study each respective market to understand what's trending in a particular area and how each market is changing so I can help my clients make informed decisions.

Continuing Education, Distinctions, Awards and Volunteering

Working in real estate provides you with many opportunities to further your specializations and define yourself as a professional. I am a member of myriad networks that require you to take classes to receive specific designations. These classes and distinctions are like getting an advanced degree in college. I am an ABR, Accredited Buyer's Representative. I'm also a CRS, Certified Residential Specialist. Out of more than 1,000,000 Realtors® in the country, less than 3% are Certified Residential Specialists. Needless to say, as a CRS, you are in the top group of all of the agents in the country.

Additionally, I'm an SRES, Senior Real Estate Specialist. My mentor, Tim Corliss, is the founder of this designation. Tim Corliss was the President of the California Association of Realtors® and President of the local Beverly Hills/Greater Los Angeles Association of Realtors®. He and I pioneered the system in the 1980s and 1990s for this designation. After several years of test marketing and fine-tuning the various components of this designation, Tim got the designation approved by the California Association of Realtors® and the National Association of Realtors®. In the process, we learned how best to serve the aging population. There are special financial considerations, as well as issues in preparing a property for sale, among others, for senior citizens when they sell their property. Sometimes they have deferred maintenance that needs to be taken care of before the sale. We help them get their property in shape to put it on the market and the preparation can be quite extensive.

I'm also a GRI, Graduate of the Realtors® Institute and a Certified Negotiator Expert (CNE). All of these designations and the education required to obtain these designations result in networking opportunities where I can expand my contacts with other Realtors® from around the world.

I'm on the Advisory Board of the Teles Foundation at Teles Properties. Our mission is to reach out to the respective communities we serve from Carmel to Coronado and Boulder, Colorado and identify organizations in need of assistance. I think it's incumbent of those who reap the benefits of their communities to give back to those in need and make a difference in peoples' lives. There are so many who need and deserve our help. Volunteering for Habitat for Humanity, building homes for those who would not otherwise have an opportunity to own their own homes is extremely rewarding. These homes are built by local volunteers as well as the people who will occupy these homes and we celebrate the end result in community.

I continue to pursue my music, singing with the Angel City Chorale, a 130+ voice non-profit chorale, bringing music to all including those on skid row, in nursing homes, the Boys and Girls Clubs of Los Angeles County, conventions and other outreach organizations. We also share our gift of music with those around the world, from Ireland (2007) to South Africa (2011) and England (2016), joining with local groups in celebrating the universal language of music.

Starting Out

When I first got my real estate license, it was overwhelming. I had never sold anything before. I had experienced the administrative side of real estate but had never been out in the field at open houses, working with potential buyers and sellers. Clients are placing their trust in you with one of the largest investments of their lifetime so I learned the importance of investigating everything that is going to affect the purchase of their property to allow me to guide them to a successful outcome.

Dealing with Adversity

From 2002-2007 I experienced a very difficult time navigating the medical field with my husband who had developed a brain tumor. We experienced many ups and downs as we gathered information and dealt with the daily challenges of living with constant change. I became the supporting spouse and was extremely thankful I had chosen to become involved in real estate. It not only gave us the financial means we needed to meet the constant and escalating medical costs, but the flexibility to deal with numerous health issues that came to light as time progressed. There were psychotic episodes and the onset of early dementia. One summer he was in a coma and fortunately came out of it, however he had to learn the basics of reading, writing and math all over again.

After two brain surgeries my husband lost his cognitive abilities and could no longer work in his chosen field. His employer gave him many options of other simpler jobs for which we were very grateful as it meant a continuation of our health benefits. Other employees also donated their vacation and sick time allowing us to maintain health benefits until his death. This meant the world to us and we were extremely appreciative. The support I received from both my son, who was still living with us at the time, as well as friends and family was enormous.

I was very vulnerable during those years and I feared clients who knew about my situation would not want to work with me. I remember one time I was being considered for a listing and one agent did use my situation against me telling the client that I had a sick husband at home and wouldn't be able to devote my full attention to the sale of their home. This was simply not true. I was working even harder to overcome any fear of my not giving anyone my full attention. Unfortunately I did not get that particular listing and it was lesson in just how competitive real estate can be and what others will say about you. Interestingly enough the year my husband died (2007), I experienced one of my best years in real estate. I had to put one foot in front of the other and keep going regardless of the adversity before me. It gave me a greater appreciation of others who face challenges of any kind and keep moving forward.

What Buyers Need to Know When Buying a Home

When I begin working with buyers I recommend they make a list of what they can and cannot live without to help them in defining their dream home. In most cases, buyers will not find 100% of what they're looking for and there will be compromises.

Figuring out the location first is paramount. Location is one thing you can never change. Then think about size, floor plans, amenities and finishes.

Some of the questions I ask clients to assist them in this process are:

- Do they have children?
- Are public schools important or do they plan on attending private schools?
- How important is their commuting time to work?
- Is access to community events important?

Location is not only important when buying but important to think about when it's time to sell as well. The floor plan is also key. You can certainly change a floor plan if a major remodel is in your budget, otherwise, the basic layout should be one that fits your lifestyle. Another consideration is the condition of the home. Do you want to move into something that doesn't need any work that will usually be priced on the higher end of a buyers range or are you willing to do a little or a lot of work that translates into a lower purchase price? Whether or not a house has been 'flipped' is something to think about. Is the house well done or were corners cut? Inspectors are key in determining if a 'flipped house' was well done or not. As a new buyer, you don't want to be paying for some else's mistakes or oversights.

Buyers often get excited about a potential property and sometimes aren't as aware of potential problems so it's extremely important to have good inspectors on whom to rely to guide you through the process. Sometimes there are significant red flags discovered during the course of an inspection and buyers need to pass on a property. The inspections give you insight into the areas of the property you can't see such as plumbing, electrical, foundation, etc. It's not easy but I always counsel clients not to get married to a home until the inspections are done and negotiated.

Real Estate Financing

When I first meet with buyers, I ask them if they have a relationship with a lender. Sometimes they do and more than often, they do not. If they do, I respect those relationships but want to insure the lenders are local so they're aware of what's happening in a particular marketplace. If they don't have a relationship I like to give them three referrals. As in any profession, working with a lender is part personality, part knowledge and what financial programs a lender has to offer.

I also let them know what documents a lender will want to see such as their last two years tax returns, current pay stubs, bank statements and so on. That way, they'll be more prepared and the approval process will often move more quickly.

I believe working with a mortgage broker is most advantageous for a buyer because they can look for the program that's right for the client and not try to make the client right for the program. They can often be more creative as well if the situation calls for it.

Financing is constantly changing. I can give a client basic guidelines but it's always best to speak with a qualified expert so I always recommend a client speak with their lender regarding their specific needs. Figure out how much of a loan you'll qualify for and what is comfortable for you in terms of monthly payments. A lender may qualify you for more than you'd like so it's important to have that conversation.

How to Sell Your Home Quickly

There are many considerations when selling your home. Homes that are de-cluttered, clean and updated usually get a higher price than those where little or no preparation is done. Ideally, if you want to sell your home quickly, you need to de-clutter. We all want to be surrounded by pictures of our families and friends and mementos of where we've been. It's a good idea to remove as many of those as possible so a prospective buyer can envision living in your home.

You also want to make sure everything is as fresh and clean as possible. Living in our homes, we're not always aware of how a prospective buyer might view our home. I recommend a fresh coat of paint if it's been awhile since you last painted. If some of the hardwood floors need sprucing up or carpeting needs to be replaced, if you are able, I recommend doing that work.

I also believe in staging a property. Again, we've lived and decorated our homes according to our needs. A stager brings a fresh perspective and is well versed in what today's buyers are looking for. They can make a room come alive with added color, or different furniture placement or perhaps recommending different furniture they have in their warehouse that might be more appealing. Most agents work closely with their stagers and there are stagers for every budget so be sure to ask your agent for recommendations. Statistics show that staged properties sell in a shorter period of time and at a higher price than those properties that are not staged.

If staging isn't in your budget, many agents will pay for a consultation with their stager. The stager will come and give a seller advice to add some colors with pillows and throws or a few pictures or accents here and there. They will work with what you have to showcase your home in the best possible light.

Sellers often think pricing is the most important component of a sale. It's certainly one of the top considerations, but it's really part of the marketing strategy as to where you position your property given the current market and what other homes your prospective buyers might be considering. Your agent will run a comparative market analysis for you, comparing your home to other similar homes in terms of age, condition, size and amenities that are currently on the market, in escrow or have sold within the past six months. You'll decide together where your home fits within that range.

Depending on your timeframe and financial goals, you can decide what the best pricing strategy is for you. There is event pricing, where you price your home just under the market to create excitement, value and hopefully elicit multiple offers. There's traditional pricing, where you price a property as close as possible to where you believe it will sell. And there's conventional pricing, where you price a property above where you believe it will sell. I usually recommend event or traditional pricing. Buyers want to see value, and in today's market, despite historically low interest rates, if you price a property too high, agents will be less inclined to show it and it could sit on the market for a while. The longer a property sits on the market, the more a buyer wonders what's wrong with it, even though there might be nothing wrong with it. Sellers put their home on the market for a reason: death, divorce, relocation, financial concerns, moving up or downsizing. Whatever the reason, if the property is not well priced and the perceived value doesn't match the property, buyers will bypass the house in favor of others or make a low offer, hoping the sellers are getting desperate. Proper pricing is essential to a successful outcome.

I recently listed a home that was previously listed with another agent for 9 months. According to my seller, the other agent convinced him he should price it at a much higher price that what he should have. It was overpriced, the price was not adjusted for several months and despite weekly open houses, there were no offers forthcoming. If a seller wants to test a price, I may not recommend it but I'm happy to try a higher price with the stipulation that if it does not sell in the first three weeks, that we adjust the price to what I initially recommended. It's a win win.

I listed the home at what I felt was a very realistic price, staged it and took new photos. It looked completely different and with a fresh approach, I was able to sell the property in multiple offers within the first two weeks of listing it. Needless to say, my seller was thrilled. There were 3 other properties on the market in a small gated community at the same time. None of the others sold because they were priced too high. Two of them have been re-listed with the same or other agents and are still on the market many months later.

Showing a Property

You never know what you'll find when you're showing property. I remember showing one condominium that was on a lock box and that I could show at any time. I walked in with my client and there were people sleeping in the living room! I was shocked and my clients and I felt very uncomfortable. I quietly apologized. The occupants said it was ok to look and so we did! It was very strange.

Prior to taking my buyers out to see property, I always ask if anyone will be home or not or if there is anything in particular I should know about a property prior to showing it. I don't like being surprised and want to prepare my clients prior to seeing a property.

When showing a listing of mine, I like to get there at least 10-15 minutes ahead of time to open windows and doors, turn on lights and spruce up a little just in case the seller has forgotten about a showing or had to rush out for some reason. I've been known to make beds, put things away, wash dishes...whatever will aide in showing the property in the best possible light. I always bring flowers as it adds a personal, welcoming touch.

If I'm representing a listing, I feel open houses are essential. It exposes the house not only to the neighbors who might have a friend or relative looking near them but also to prospective buyers on a larger scale than an independent showing. Sometimes neighbors want validation as to the value of their own home whether they're contemplating a move or are just curious. Either way, you never know where a conversation may lead. When a home is first listed, I usually like to hold a house open on a Sunday, then on a Tuesday for Broker's Caravan and then the following Sunday to fully expose the home to the market. After that, it depends on the activity and the sellers schedule as to whether or not additional open houses can be scheduled.

Most buyers begin their search online. Sometimes, if people want a specific neighborhood, they'll drive around to see if there are any available homes not knowing if a home has a scheduled open house or not. You never know who's going to walk into your open house and say, "Wow! I didn't think I could get into this neighborhood", or, "My agent didn't tell me about this one!"

Another reason I love what I do is that I'm a people person. I enjoy meeting new people, identifying their needs and help them fill that need. Many clients have become good friends and I welcome that opportunity. One client who I helped with two properties asked me to be the Godmother of their second daughter. I was incredibly honored. She has, aside from my daughter-in-law, become the daughter I never had. We have a very special connection not only through connecting with her parents through real estate but she has become a cellist. Music fills our souls and furthers our connection. The rewards are endless.

Marketing Real Estate

I have a detailed marketing plan I share with each prospective seller that includes my action plan from the day we sign the listing to the day we close escrow. If there are certain marketing points the seller feels are important, I make sure they're incorporated into my plan to ensure a smooth execution and a successful campaign.

There are numerous touch points I execute in bringing a new listing to market. I have an extensive pre-launch campaign that includes a Coming Soon sign, an internet countdown to arriving on the multiple listing service, a notification on several mastermind group websites, staging and several other items that build anticipation and excitement. Some of those touch points include inviting the immediate neighbors to a sneak preview or the first open house. Whether the neighbors are interested in seeing what's happening in the neighborhood or are contemplating a move or know of someone who wants to live nearby, it's important to reach out to the community.

Even though statistics show that print advertising only accounts for approximately 2% of a buyers' search, I feel it's important to advertise in the local media, so I include print advertising in my marketing plan. In addition, my company syndicates it's on-line advertising to over 17 real estate sites and includes translations into a number of foreign languages and live chat to reach out to as many interested parties as possible. Each listing has it's own web site address where all the pertinent information can be accessed including photos, school information, area maps, etc.

In addition, I belong to a variety of networking and other professional groups who meet weekly, monthly or quarterly from different companies and geographical areas to share information about our respective buyers and sellers, further expanding my reach on behalf of my clients. Eblasts are another important component of my marketing to reach my present and past clients, to make them aware of opportunities and to reach agents throughout the area to let them know about new listings and open houses. Teles Properties alone has expanded to 19 offices in just over 8 years in business from San Francisco to San Diego, including Boulder, Colorado and internationally. This is in addition to the extensive Realtor® lists we've created throughout our respective geographical areas.

Cross marketing is a unique tool we use to share our information with our associates' clients. Anyone in our company can market my property to their own database thus expanding the reach of that listing to thousands of additional potential buyers. Social media also plays an important part in my marketing plan, as that's where the millennials of today communicate.

Increasing the Value of Your Home

There are numerous ways to increase the value of your home given its current condition. It may not need anything if it's been recently remodeled. But many times homeowners defer maintenance of a property for one reason or another, be it finances, timing, indecision, etc. Curb appeal is of the utmost importance. You only get one chance to make a first impression. The more appealing your home is at first glance, the more prospective buyers will want to tour the interior of the home.

Simple things such as landscaping and painting can make a tremendous difference and often prove less expensive than anticipated. New flooring such as carpeting can also add to the overall appeal of a property.

One the of the easiest and most important things a seller can do to prepare their home for market is to make sure it's clean, including the windows and if necessary, power washing the exterior and de-clutter, with personal belongings put away including personal photographs. You want prospective buyers to be able to visualize themselves living in your home. The less personalization, the better.

Clients often ask me if they should update a kitchen or a bathroom. That's a tough decision. Kitchen and baths are the most expensive updates a seller can make. If they've already been done, buyers feel they can move right in without having to spend additional money and time in making these changes. Many buyers are happy to pay more money for these upgrades. However, unless the kitchen or bath is in really bad condition when you're ready to sell, it's best to allow a new homeowner to put their own mark on their new home once they move in. It's something you need to take into account in pricing a property if it needs to be done.

I also recommend sellers make sure everything is in working order, if possible. Make sure there are no leaks in the plumbing or problems with any of the main systems of the property. If the refrigerator is on the fritz or the microwave isn't working, get them repaired prior to coming to market. You want to present your property in the best possible light.

Why Use a Real Estate Agent?

Your property is usually the largest investment you own. You usually engage the services of experts such as attorneys, CPAs, doctors, etc. to take care of your various medical and business needs. Why not a Realtor®? There's so much to take into consideration that you may or may not be aware of including disclosures and financial considerations. Disclosures are there to protect a seller and make a buyer aware of important things to consider when deciding to purchase a property. An arms length transaction is always best so everyone feels information is being communicated and shared in a manner to allow everyone the opportunity to make an informed decision.

It's also an emotional transaction. Negotiations can often get heated so it's better to have some else do the negotiating for you. A neutral third party takes the emotion out of the negotiating, allowing everyones' voice to be heard.

In addition, as a Realtor®, I can reach thousands more people with my marketing than an individual selling their own property. My experience has also allowed me to develop safeguards to ensure a transaction does not fall out of escrow unnecessarily. I confirm a buyers' ability to purchase through their lender of choice, making sure there are no apparent red flags, double-checking with my own in-house financial arm. I have a manager, a legal department, marketing department, escrow department and other safeguards at my disposal. My support team, with whom I have worked for many years and trust, work diligently with me to ensure a smooth and seamless transition.

My Process From Start to Finish

Selling real estate is one the most stressful transactions an individual can make in their lives. It's important to hire someone in whom they place their confidence and trust in executing every step from start to finish.

- Initial meeting with client to see the property and discuss the process and marketing strategies
- Fill out the listing paperwork including disclosures for the prospective buyer
- Decide on a marketing strategy to determine the asking price
- Prepare the property for market to include de-cluttering, painting or any other necessary preparation, staging if possible
- Professional photographs taken

- Order property brochure including selecting photographs and writing copy
- Place ads in appropriate print
- Order sign up on property including Coming Soon rider 2 weeks prior to going on the market
- Organize and hold open houses and broker caravans
- Give clients feedback from each open house
- Schedule showings
- Give clients feedback from individual showings
- Respond to any and all offers
- Confirm financing with buyers lender
- Open escrow
- Confirm deposit received in escrow
- Approve escrow instructions
- Confirm City Report has been ordered
- Coordinate inspections with buyers agent
- Negotiate inspection findings. (The buyer might ask for certain things to be repaired or for a monetary credit to make repairs after the close of escrow.)
- Meet appraiser at the property and provide comparable sales
- Once everything is negotiated, ensure the buyers remove their inspection contingencies. (Contingencies are negotiated at the time of the offer. Buyers must adhere to the respective contingency timeframes or face the potential loss of their earnest money deposit.)
- Keep in touch with the buyers lender to make sure the loan process is proceeding as it should
- Assist the sellers in obtaining moving quotes and assist in arranging for moving company
- Schedule the transference of utilities
- Make sure all of the escrow requirements have been met and all paperwork has been fully executed
- Make sure loan documents have been ordered in a timely manner
- Recommend sellers fill out a forwarding address form for the post office
- Confirm escrow has scheduled time for loan documents to be signed

- Confirm home warranty has been ordered
- Confirm remaining funds have been wired to escrow in time to close
- Schedule the final walk through within five days before the close of escrow to make sure the house is in the same condition as when the buyer first made their offer; that any items that were to have been repaired have been repaired and receipts have been provided to the buyers for those repairs.
- Confirm loan has funded the day before close of escrow and convey to all parties
- Confirm all keys have been given to listing agent including any warranties or booklets and any vendors' names and phone numbers.
- Confirm property is, at a minimum, broom clean, and no debris has been left.
- If, for some reason, debris has been left behind, I call a hauler and/or charity to remove any unclaimed items.
- Upon confirmation of the recordation, give keys and any other pertinent information to buyers.
- Schedule a celebratory dinner with the sellers.

I appreciate the opportunity my clients give me in trusting me to guide them through one of the largest investments they will make in their lives. I take my responsibility very seriously, striving to ensure a thorough and smooth process, giving them as much information as possible to allow them to make informed decisions. My ultimate goal is to make sure my clients are happy about the decision they've made and enjoy the end result.

About the Author

Stacy Young

Teles Properties
Brentwood, CA

Phone: 310-367-7654
Stacyyoung.telesproporties.com

For Stacy Blair Young, the real estate business is about one thing: people. "Relationships and information are the two most important elements in any real estate transaction. I enjoy creating these relationships, hopefully on a long-term basis. I strive to make a difference in the quality of people's lives. Whether they're selling or buying, they need to know about today's market conditions and what to expect. They need a good listener, the right strategy, expert negotiating skills and someone in whom they can place their trust with one of the biggest investments of their lives. It's exciting to work with clients, figure out our approach and then make it happen."

Originally from Westport, Connecticut, Stacy is a graduate of the University of the Pacific in Stockton, California. She also studied at the University of Vienna and the Vienna Conservatory of Music in Austria. A Westside resident since the 1960s, she began her real estate career as an administrative assistant right out of college, quickly working her way up to Operations Manager, overseeing 13 offices and then Sr. Vice President of Marketing for 17 offices, gaining valuable experience along the way. She had accumulated a vast array of real estate knowledge. By the time she decided to get her license, she had a clear vision of the real estate process and had observed, first hand, numerous real estate cycles including many peaks and valleys. Since then, she has gone on to receive myriad accolades within the real estate industry and enduring loyalty and praise from her clients and peers.

If Stacy's professional expertise sounds good, you should hear her voice! Since the 1970s, Stacy has been a soloist with local symphonies and musical groups, performing both sacred and secular repertoire. She continues to sing and tour with local groups including the renowned Angel City Chorale. Giving back to her community is also an important component of Stacy's life. She performs with the Angel City Chorale in their annual Tour Of Hope, reaching out to the homeless recovering and aged in our community. She also donates her time to Habitat for Humanity and is on the Advisory Board of the Teles Foundation.

If you're going to stand up there and sing, you have to be able to hit the right notes and convey a message. It's the same with real estate. You need to listen carefully, identify the goal, create a plan, execute it and celebrate the outcome. Enjoy the process and your audience.

Perseverance Counts

By Cecily Tippery

Before real estate, I worked with numbers most of my life and eventually became a corporate Controller; my mother was a bookkeeper after all. But life changes. As part of getting my MBA, I took an aptitude test which told me I should not be working as a "bean counter;" rather, my strength lay in sales. One day, during a garage sale, a friend and Realtor®, saw me in action pointing out bargains and essentially "selling." He said, "You'd be really good in real estate" and he encouraged me to consider that as a career. Later, I started working for my Broker friend as an Office Manager and he again encouraged me to get my license. I thought about it and decided it was worth a try.

In my first year, my W-9 reported a whopping $12,000 and then I had to pay back $3,500 to unemployment! It was a bit disheartening, but I kept going. At that time, in San Jose, the REO (Real Estate Owned) sales started to pick up. The Broker suggested calling lenders directly. Because of my corporate background I could speak intelligently with bankers and I understood corporations. So, I just began prospecting – created a binder with all my contacts and a compiled a record of conversations; a hand-written data base. I called "the bank" whenever one of their properties went into foreclosure. After calling one woman about 15 times, she finally said, "Okay, I got this property, do you want it?" So that was my first actual sale after taking about four months of calling and being persistent.

Later, she told me, "You said the value of it was $185,000. My appraiser said it was $170,000. So I went with you." As I recall, we listed it for $185,000 and we finally sold it for $182,000. That was in 1991, which was the beginning of an uptick in foreclosures.

I learned that as long as you have the same phone number and email, the banks will keep your information in their data base and contact you as long as you have done a good job. So I keep the same phone number, the same email, and keep my name active and updated with various companies. This contributed to my success greatly in 2008 and after.

Contrary to many people, 2007 through 2011 were stellar years for me. I was in the Top 10 Teams nationally in total units for Coldwell Banker in 2008. My team of 12 sold approximately 300 homes in 2008, then 185 homes 2009, and 165 in 2010. Over my career, over 1000 homes have changed hands where I and/or my team have represented either the Buyer or the Seller.

The Default Industry

I have been doing bank foreclosures almost my entire career. The market goes up but when it goes down, it is good for me. There are several organizations which focus on that segment of the real estate industry and have been helpful both in terms of contacts but also education. REOMAC, primarily an association of mortgage default service professionals, was the first organization I joined as an affiliate partner. Second is the National Association of Real Estate Brokers which is a group of Real Estate professionals who work in the foreclosure business. Five Star came along a bit later which is primarily an education arena for default professionals.

A lot of agents look down on REO and bank foreclosures because they are typically not in as good of condition as an owner occupied home. There is a reason it is in foreclosure. Sadly, it is often because someone lost their job or there have been health problems. Generally, the owner does not have the money to take care of repairs and maintenance. You have to be empathetic to their situation when you are speaking with them. Being in that circumstance for whatever reason, of course, causes stress. You have to understand and only push where you can push and back off when necessary.

I Shortened My Commute

In 1991, my "eventual" husband and I moved in together in Discovery Bay and were married in 1998. The good thing about real estate is you can take it with you wherever you go.

At that time, I was working in San Jose and Fremont but living in Pleasanton and then Discovery Bay. As the commute could be as long as 2 hours one way, my focus changed to the territory between Pittsburg and Discovery Bay. I just followed Highway 4 across East Contra Costa County which is also the geographic bounds of my Association of Realtors®. Because I know the Pleasanton and Livermore markets, I also included that in my zip code areas when soliciting foreclosure properties. You have to be careful as an REO agent because you are responsible to check your properties every week to ensure there are no break-ins, vandalism, or health and safety issues. As the clients often say, we agents "are their eyes and ears."

Last year, the percentage of my listings that were foreclosures was about 50%. This year that probably will not be the case as we are still on a foreclosure downturn. I am working on my traditional client database.

I have been a listing agent for so long, it is hard for me to change my hat and represent a buyer, particularly on a foreclosure. An investor needs to make money, so they come in as low as they can and of course the bank wants to sell it as high as they can. On all my listings, I choose not to be a dual agent and so I normally do not market to investors or those buyers who want to work with the listing agent only.

East Contra Costa County

We have seven cities here in this little geographic area and they are all uniquely different. I lived in Seattle for a time and it sort of reminds me of the very distinct districts found there. We have something for everyone here in East Contra Costa County. Cities include Pittsburg/Bay Point, Bethel Island, Knightsen, Oakley, Antioch, Brentwood and Discovery Bay which is primarily a resort community. There is water access to San Francisco bay and you could sail around the world from your own backyard and return home right to your own back door. People live here for the resort atmosphere and the boating. When you are showing property here, I always get the question "How far is it to fast water?" My most popular and informative response is, "It is one or two cans of your favorite beverage."

Getting Involved

I became a Women's Council of Realtors® member simply because when I moved to this community I thought this was a good way to get to know people. After being a member for a while, I recall going to a retreat in Santa Cruz for a day and Jim Hamilton, then President of the California Association of Realtors®, urged all of us as potential leaders to get involved with our local associations. So, I got involved in the Education Committee at the Delta Association of Realtors®. I also volunteered for Project Second Chance to help tutor English as a second language. The Board of Directors named me member of the year in 2006 – I do not know why they did that but that was a great honor! That award sort of galvanized me to think, "Maybe I can contribute differently and on a different level." I continued my board membership and work in Women's Council of Realtors®. Everything came together in 2010, when I was elected President of the Delta Association of Realtors®. Eventually, this led to being elected President of Women's Council of Realtors® California coming up in 2016.

Why Being a Realtor® Matters

It is important to remember the difference between a licensee and a Realtor®. Almost anyone can get a real estate license. It takes several college credit courses, you pass a test and you get your license. Some people take their brokers exam right away, but I studied and became a Broker later in 2012. Once you get your license, you are officially a licensed real estate agent, but this does not make you a Realtor®. By joining a firm that belongs to a Board or Association of

Realtors®, you automatically become a Realtor® with the California Association of Realtors® and the National Association of Realtors®.

This is important because there is a Code of Ethics that Realtors® subscribe to that include a set of professional standards. A licensee – someone who is a real estate agent but not a Realtor® - does not have to do that. The National Association of Realtors® is also working on a Commitment to Excellence that will further differentiate licensees from Realtors®.

This is really important for consumers to understand. In my listing presentation, I include a copy of my license and a copy of the Code of Ethics, which explains our duties as professional real estate agents. The National Association of Realtors® was started in 1906 so people were accountable to the industry. We have a long and proud history of service to our clients and our communities.

Selling Your Home

When selling your home one of the first things you need to do is find the right Realtor® for you. Not every Realtor® and every client are going to be a good fit; you are creating a short-term business partnership. It is all about that communication – the vibe – between client and Realtor®. Do you feel good with this person? Do you trust them? How do they show you they trust you? What is your conversation? It is a two way street. It is not all about money - forget the money. For me it is more about "Am I going to get along well with this person?"

If you do not price the property right, no matter what you do it is not going to sell. So that is why as the professional, the business partnership is critical. With an REO listing and with a traditional client you give them your opinion of value and they decide. The difference is that you can look a local Seller in the eye and discuss a strategy.

The marketing plan depends on the property. I might advertise in the Wall Street Journal or in a magazine for a particular property simply because it might reach a different set of buyers. Mostly the marketing is through the multiple listing service, local signs, and networking. Our listings go on to Realtor.com, Trulia.com and on the internet on the major sites. In the first quarter in 2015, in my market, we sold approximately 800 homes and approximately 88% of them were Broker to Broker. This demonstrates the need to reach the right agents. A buyer may call the listing agent first, because they saw the home on the internet or a sign, but they usually have an agent who will represent them, so it is important to reach a buyer where ever or how ever they may be looking. I always try to do an open house at least once if the seller will let me because I want to see what the buyers are thinking and saying. I always think about who is going to buy that property and how we are going to reach them.

Depending on the situation, I either take my own photos of the property or often use a professional photographer. Photos are an ideal marketing technique - I want to use the brightest and best photos I can. I usually try to put some flowers or foliage somewhere in the photos. Sometimes, just by changing the angle and putting something different in the photo, it looks a little more inviting. It also helps to change out a photo here and there to keep the property fresh.

Move it Fast

The best way to attract a Buyer quickly is to clean and get rid of everything the Seller absolutely does not need or want. I had a property once that was fairly dark inside - a lot of shutters and darker decorator paint colors. It took the Seller a couple of weeks to get it clean, de-clutter everything, and take everything away they did not need. They also made a few repairs. They had three garage sales and packed everything else up. When we finally got an accepted offer, the Buyer was really negative; very verbal about all the things that needed changing, what was wrong with the house and on and on. This Buyer finally backed out - just canceled the contract - which was a relief to all of us. After that – this is going to sound strange - but I went through the entire house with a bell to clear it of the negative energy. I said to the Sellers, "I do not want you to think I am crazy but the bells' vibrations will clear the house." I just walked through the house ringing the bell. About a week later we got a really good offer; the new Buyers loved the house and everything worked just like it was supposed to!

The house has to help you. Even in a foreclosure, I say to the house, "I need your help. I need you to help me find a new owner that is going to take care of you." That may sound really weird but I do say that and when I am walking through a house, I touch and talk to it, to make sure it knows I am there for it.

The best way to attract a Buyer is price. I tell Sellers to do what you need to do to get your home ready, but price is the main thing. You do not want to miss the Buyer that cannot afford the higher price and does not see your home because it is overpriced. You also need to choose the right Realtor®; one that you trust, you can work with, and who communicates well with you. Get some references before you choose. Once, I had a guy who ran me through the ringer. After interviewing five times – I was up against some really tough competition, they finally made the decision to go with me. That taught me to be prepared, be open and show I have a sense of humor.

When choosing a Realtor®, I suggest a Homeowner or a Buyer ask an agent about how they communicate to make sure they are on the same wavelength. The Agent needs to be adaptable but still keep up their processes and systems so that something does not fall through the cracks. If the person is not digitally savvy, the agent needs to know they are going to be spending more time at the house reviewing paperwork and strategy. The Seller and Buyer should consider asking questions like:

- How often are you going to communicate?

- What sort of communication process do you have?

- What are you going to do to show this home or market this home?

- What sort of team or back-up do you have?

There always should be a discussion about price; I always ask, "What do you think the value is and why?" Then they are going to tell me all the reasons they like the house and what makes it different. I would advise a Seller to ask the Agent to take them around to other homes. I know when I go look at a newly staged beautiful house and then come back to my house I see all the things I could change.

My Process

I usually send out a prelisting package so my clients have some idea of what to expect. I even do that with Buyers if I can. To the Seller, I deliver information about marketing strategy that explains how the market works and why they need to price it right and possible strategies. I often will include my market analysis without a pre determined value. I just slip in a page or two about the competition, pending and sold homes in the area. I will give that to them upfront, at least one day before I meet them at their home.

I include a page about "What are your expectations from a Realtor®?" and "Why did you buy this home?" and "What attracted you to this home?" So they can think about that and we can create a conversation about it. I include a page about me and my team; this includes a transaction coordinator as well as agents in my company. In addition, there is a little bit about my company, company values, and my mission statement. If I can, I will take a picture of the house or download one from Google and put it on the front cover. I might even include a sample flier.

Everything is done upfront before I even have the listing. If I expect to take the listing at the appointment, I will bring all the paperwork with me. If it is a two step listing, I will just talk with them and I give them sample contracts and a little bit about disclosures so they are prepared. The actual listing appointment takes a couple of hours for them to complete the disclosures and do all the paperwork.

Talking with the client about their home, educating and a bit of sparring about price is expected and the best conversation. I like talking to people about how to market their home. I think it is fun to walk through someone's house and say, "Oh if we move this over here or maybe move this here add a couple of plants and remove this then it will open up the room." Having a Theater Arts degree helps me visually; I started out in scene design so although I am not an official stager, I can give my clients an idea of what a buyer may want to see. Having also directed and acted in plays, I guess I like running the show!

I am a little concerned about this digital world where we just send things for people to sign over the internet. There is a lot of small print on those documents and I want to make sure the client understands what he or she is signing. That is why I like going over to someone's house to look them in the eye, face to face. Then I know they understand and they can ask whatever questions they want and feel comfortable doing so. If I cannot physically see them, then expect long phone calls! Talking with them, gives me a second look at the paperwork, too. When I first started in real estate, I remember waking up in the middle of the night, thinking, "Did I check that box correctly on that contract?"

Most people do not buy or sell more than three or four homes in their lifetime. If something goes wrong, they want to blame someone and usually the Realtor® is brought into it. As a Realtor®, I facilitate, advise and consult. I cannot tell my client what to do, but I can give advice. When I am asked directly, I give my opinion. The Clients make the choices and the decisions whether they are a bank or a traditional Seller or Buyer. There was one house where I was representing a Buyer. We looked at it and she really liked it. I should have just gone over and said, "This is the house you need to buy. Do not look at another one. Just buy this one." She did not buy it but she told me a couple of years later, "You know I think about that house quite a bit." And I responded, "I knew you should have purchased it. We should have made an offer that day." And she said, "I wish we had," and again it is just one of those things you wish you had said and maybe it would have made a difference, however, it was always her decision.

To be successful in real estate you need perseverance. You keep doing what you think you need to do to succeed and it changes but the basics remain the same. I have a coach that keeps me galvanized. You have to focus on your business not just doing your business. Because I was a Controller, I was used to processes and systems and I like that about real estate. It is hard to translate systems, create and monitor them as you have to do this as a business owner or pay for someone to help you.

Perseverance: it is being in the same market with the same phone number and email for a length of time. It is a little bit of luck but also staying the course and keeping your head up and always moving forward. To succeed in real estate you have to be prepared and positive.

About the Author

Cecily Tippery

Office: (925) 634-7820
Mobile: (925) 640-6698
www.Cecily.com
Email: RealEstate@Cecily.com

Cecily Tippery has been a Realtors® ince November, 1990, the year before she earned her MBA from San Jose State University. Previously, she worked as a corporate Controller in Boise Idaho, Seattle Washington and San Jose California. Cecily grew up in Boise and was active in local theatre productions both on and behind the stage, earning a BA in Theatre Arts from Boise State College, soon to be Boise State University, home of the now nationally ranked Bronco football team.

Cecily and Craig have a son, Justin, who lives in San Francisco and who works in Corporate sales. Her husband Craig Klooster is a podiatrist with offices in Stockton and Pleasanton. They live in Discovery Bay and enjoy water sports, boating, and wine tasting. They have two Kerry Blue Terriers: Toby and Sophie. Cecily is passionate about abandoned and missing pets.

As a Top Producer in the industry, Cecily chose to be more active in her Association. She has been a Director since 2006 and was awarded Member of the Year that same year. She was President in 2010 and is currently Region 5 Chair at the California Association of Realtors®. A member of Women's Council of Realtors® since 2002, Cecily has held the position of President of the Delta Chapter as well as State District Vice President and Governor; she was awarded State Member of the Year in 2011, and is currently serving as President-elect of the Women's Council of Realtors® California.

My Real Estate Story

By Roy Tedsen

I have been a licensed Real Estate Agent/Broker for over 37 years. However, even before my real estate career, I was active in a number of relative fields that could arguably be interpreted as being real estate related.

My father was a dairy farmer and real estate developer. He introduced my brother and me to hard work early on in my development. We worked a full day out on the dairy and then after dinner, often times worked several more hours on whatever project he happened to be working on; clearing land, fixing up, painting, landscaping, and doing whatever it took to make the project successful.

After that background growing up and then the practical experience afforded me through financial institutions, land use planning, development work, project processing, teaching at College of the Redwoods and Anthony Schools and then my own personal projects, a career in real estate seemed like a natural fit.

After I graduated with a degree in Business from Southern Oregon College (now SOU Southern Oregon University), I then went on to work initially as a management trainee for Jackson County

Federal Savings and Loan Association. After being laid off due to a dramatic shift in the economy, I left the Rogue Valley and came back to the coast to begin an entry level position with the Del Norte County Planning Department as a Planning Technician. I worked my way up through the various ranks to complete my planning career as Planning Director Pro-Tem, and then leaving public service to go into the private sector starting a new company by the name of "NorthWest Demographics." NWD did project processing and wrote environmental impact reports. I also worked for Simonson Lumber Co. to do "Development Propensity Reports" for all of their holdings because they were negotiating at the time to sell their vast timber lands to Arcata Redwoods Corp. and the owner, Lee Simonson wanted to determine "highest and best use" for all of the property he controlled. Since I could see that I was basically working myself out of a job, I decided to go into the real estate business. Because I was so apprehensive about totally depending upon commission sales for our income, I also worked for Anthony Schools, a license prep. school and College of the Redwoods, teaching business courses and real estate classes. At the same time, I was doing appraisal work, initially residential and then commercial real estate as well.

My real estate firm services all of Del Norte County, although my commercial work encompasses all of the Pacific Northwest. I have done commercial real estate transactions as far away as Helena Montana/ Coeur D'Alene, Idaho to the east and north to Washington, all throughout Oregon and as far south as Santa Maria, California.

What's great about my community?

Crescent City is a very unique place indeed! We are logistically removed from any other major market. It is 85 miles to Eureka, California, 83 miles to Grants Pass, Oregon and we are 26 miles south of Brookings, Oregon. The community is very rural and up until about 20 years ago, we depended upon the timber and fishing industries to survive. Today, the timber industry is all but gone, but fishing still plays a major role in our local economy and government is the biggest employer in Del Norte County.

What is so great about Del Norte County is the unmitigated natural beauty. Most people who travel up this way think that San Francisco is "Northern California." That to us is Central California. San

Francisco is over 356 miles south of our little coastal town and most of the people there don't even know we exist.

Over 83% of the county is either National Forest lands/National Parks/State Parks and of the remainder, over half is in the "Timber Preserve Zones" where the only use is the growing and harvesting of timber. Of the remainder, over half is in either "Prime Agricultural" lands or "Riparian Habitat." So, as you can see there is not much property for development.

We do so much more than sell homes

In a rural area like Crescent City, it is important to cover the full spectrum of real estate. Our firm is unique in that regard because we do so much more than just selling homes. We have a build to suit program, we build spec homes, we buy/remodel homes, we make real estate loans, we have a full service property management program, and we can assist in development projects and have done numerous subdivisions and commercial developments. We have helped people with real estate consulting and I have been called upon several times to testify in court as an "expert witness."

I have been fortunate to be the most consistent recipient of the "Multi-Million Dollar Club" award in the history of Del Norte Association of Realtors® (I have 36 real estate awards on the wall), I am the founder and chairman of "Our Daily Bread Ministries" Advisory Committee and I'm a charter member and former president of the Del Norte Tennis Association. What also keeps me busy is playing bass with the Praise Team at Grace Lutheran Church and I was a former member, Ranger #6 of the Dixieland Rangers, a 14 member jazz band that participates in many of the local community events.

Lessons Learned

When I first got into the real estate business, I was young and idealistic and overzealous and all of those things, and even though I was raised a Christian, I thought at the time that God was in church and once you walked out the door that it was no holds barred and business was business. That was my thought back then.

I was working with a gentleman and his wife, who were referred to me by a previous client. I knew that they were very religious people. The first thing you do, of course, when you're working with someone, is to qualify them to find out what they can afford. This family wanted to look at large acreage farms, because they had children and they wanted to raise them in a rural environment. True to my responsibility as an agent, we went out, and we looked at several farms, but as we were doing that, I was asking them questions. I got the same response from them "God is going to open the doors for us." I'd piggyback off of one question after another to try to get a handle on what they could afford and whether or not they could purchase anything. Sadly, it was starting to look like I was going to have a rough day as I was going to waste a lot of my time. With the facts I was able to uncover about their financial situation, it seemed they would never afford what they wanted. They were adamant that God was going to take care of them and I eventually told them, "Well you know what? Sometimes God's busy with other things, and he doesn't get involved in real estate."

In total, I showed them four farms and there was one in particular that they were very enthusiastic about. They absolutely loved it and I kept thinking, "Well, this is working very well, but I know they can't afford it..." So we walked around the property. We walked into the barn. We walked around the fields. It had the ethos that they were looking for to raise their family. They wanted to be a family that was self-reliant. They wanted to have their church and their family and to be a close-knit group. And it had all of the amenities that they were looking for.

It was a funky old farmhouse. And it had a nice, big barn on it. The house was at least 50 years old, and the barn looked even older than that. There was a lot of work that needed to be done, but that lit their fire even more because that's what they wanted to do. Eventually the kids spread out. The mom went this way. The husband kind of went along with me, and we talked about all the things that they were going to do and the kids kept running back to us, and I could just feel the momentum that was building. And the more momentum that built, the more I felt I was doing them an extreme disservice because I knew they couldn't afford this property.

I started to feel really bad for them. At one point, I was standing by the fence, and I was looking out into this beautiful pastoral setting.

The sun was starting to set and I was starting to think, "Roy, what are you doing?" Just then, the husband walked up to me, and he put his hand on my shoulder. He said, "Roy, I want you to come into the barn with us." I thought, "Oh, okay. They probably have some questions about the structural stability of the barn or something." But as we walked to the barn, he said, "Roy, I want you to pray with us." I thought, "Oh, no. I don't want to pray about this. This is ridiculous. You can't buy the property and we're going to go have to pray?" I begrudgingly went into the barn, and there was the whole family in a circle on their knees in the straw. The husband brings me over, and we all hold hands. As we're gathered in this circle, the barn swallows are flying through, chirping. The sun's going down, and a shaft of light is coming through the barn. I'm thinking, "Oh my goodness. This is horrible. They can't afford this property!"

The husband leads the family in prayer. And a tremor travels up my spine. I start thinking, "You know? Maybe God could make this happen." After the prayer, we walked out, and I was thinking, "Well, that was kind of cool." So I asked him some more questions, and he tells me he's a veteran. And I thought, "Well, how about CalVet?" And then I realized he can't purchase through CalVet because CalVet's out of funds.

I went back to my office and I started working on it. I was filled with doubt, of course. But the husband kept telling me, "Hey, God has determined we are going to buy this property." I kept smiling and saying, "Well, we'll give it a shot, but…"The husband kept saying, "Roy, you'll see." Unbeknownst to me, the legislature had just authorized new funding for CalVet! Things were looking up.

But then we had several other hurdles to get through. The closest CalVet appraiser was located in Redding. It's almost impossible to get him to come to Crescent City because he's too busy over in Redding and it's a four hour drive. When I called over there to the VA office and talked to them hoping to convince the appraiser to come for this family they said, "You know what? The appraiser is scheduled to do another appraisal over there in your area tomorrow and we can just add yours on!"

There was another problem. The family did not have any down payment whatsoever. However, suddenly the husband calls me and said, "I got a call from my wife's mother and father, they heard about our purchase, and they are going to gift us the money that we need in order to make the purchase."

It was like that the whole way through. Every time I had an obstacle, the door just went flying open. They bought the farm and I came to realize through that situation that God is involved in real estate and everything else.

Our own investment story

When my wife and I first moved back to Crescent City, we bought our first house on Anzio Street. It was a 993 square foot, three bedroom, one bath house with a single car garage that had been built in 1952 and it was in a VA/FHA construction project. The house was really derelict at the time; it needed a new roof, new windows, new floors and a new garage door among other things. We called it the Halloween house because it was painted orange and was ugly. The lawn was clear up to my waist! My wife and I fixed it up and lived there for about two and a half years; the whole time we never had any furniture except for a twin bed that my mother and father gave to us. We never even had a refrigerator or a stove. We cooked off of a hot plate, and if we bought anything cold, we had a cement sink out in the garage, and that's where we stored our milk.

We bought it for $16,000 and two years later we sold it for $27,000. That was the catalyst for our being able to step up into another house. The next house we bought was 1,200 square feet, and it was also in rough shape, but it had an ocean view and we knew we could turn it into something great. We actually turned it into a 3,200 square foot home that was two-storey and had a mother-in-law's quarters and detached double car garage. We designed the house around the view. The home is currently being used as a bed and breakfast.

The next property we purchased was a commercial property, and the rest is history; we just kept investing. I worked with the builder on that first job, and I did the design work myself. My deal with the builder was that he would allow me to help him do the construction and give me credit for any sweat equity that I was able to provide the property. Because of that, I was able to garner a very good equity position.

I was fortunate that my wife always had a job in teaching which afforded us the base income. Throughout our investment career, our pact was that we never use the money that I was able to make for any monthly bills.

Solid Advice:

One day in the early 1980's my wife's friend came to me and asked for some real estate advice. They were extremely cautious, conservative people, and they never owned a home. Neither of their parents had owned their own home either, and they always rented. But they were curious about what we were doing and started asking questions. They were personal friends, so I was very hesitant about introducing them to the world of investing and real estate. They were intrigued by what we were doing and wanted to know more, so I decided to embark on the challenge. I kept telling them all along, "Real estate is a long-term investment" and I showed them a project that I thought they should invest in. It was a development with one acre lots and the cost was $26,000 for the undeveloped 1 acre parcel in the redwoods. Before he bought, he said to me "Roy, my wife and I have talked about this and we are really afraid. The only way we are going to go ahead with this is if you give us a personal guarantee that this is going to be successful."

I said, "Well, I don't normally do this, but let me think about it." So I talked to my wife and then went back to him and I said, "OK, as my friend I will give you my personal guarantee that this will be a successful project for you. However, there's one caveat; you have to hold this long term. This cannot be a quick turnover for you. This has to be your home. This has to be where you and your wife live and where you raise your family." At that point, they hadn't even started their family yet but they agreed. So I set him up with a builder and we did a build-to-suit. He built a 2,200 square foot, three bedroom, two bath with a double car garage. The total cost for the construction was $86,000. He had roughly $112,000 into it. With the miscellaneous landscaping work, putting in the roads, clearing and everything else he had another $10,000 invested. He was into it with a cost basis of $122,000 at the time. They lived there their entire marriage and raised three children in that home.

143

The other thing I told them up front when I gave them the guarantee, was "front loading." When they borrowed the money for the loan, they borrowed an extra $10,000 and they front loaded. In other words, by paying the $10,000 as their first payment they completely gutted the interest rate for their amortized loan. Normally, for the first 10 years of payments when you make your payment, 99% of it goes toward interest, and it takes a long time to build equity in the property. But since they front loaded, all of a sudden, they were way ahead. I also counseled them to amortize it over 30 years. And instead of paying the minimum payment, to pay double the payment because they could since they were a double income family. Also, instead of paying on the 15th when their payment was due, to pay on the 1st, before it was due. And so following my advice they build equity very quickly. They had their house paid off in under 14 years. And they owned it free and clear. Sadly, after owning the property for over 30 years, the wife died of cancer. It was too sad for the husband to continue living there without her, so he sold it last year for $325,000.

At the close of escrow, he told me something that really made me feel good. He put his hand on my shoulder and looked me in the eye, and said, "Roy, you were true to your word." That was very gratifying to me. There are many horror stories in the last decade of people buying homes and losing money, but if you do it right, buy at the right time and hold onto the property long term real estate can still be a positive investment.

It is crucial to have cash flow. I regard each property in its own bucket. I use the term buckets. Each property has to be able to be self-sustaining and stand on its own in its own bucket.

Today we own several units. Some of the properties we own are multifamily, but most of the units are free standing homes. We have some commercial properties as well. Earlier, I mentioned the ocean front property that I sold, the one that is now a B&B. The reason I sold it was we had an opportunity to get into an 18,000 square foot grocery store, and it is now leased on a long-term basis to a Grocer (a national retailer). It's a full city block at high exposure frontage in our area's premier commercial corridor. They maintain the building and the parking lot and we're afforded a very good income from that one investment. Even though this property was a good investment, we sold it! Why? Because building a real estate investment portfolio is opportunistic; when you see the right move, you can't be married to any specific property, you have to be ready to move. Never get emotionally attached to a piece of real estate-it is a commodity. You need to use the commodity so that it serves your investment strategy best!

Basically, I believe in buying for the long term, and building, slowly, a quality portfolio. However, here are some reasons to sell: fluctuations in the economy (if a property has a negative cash-flow and it looks like we're headed for a "deceleration period") you need to bolster cash for an unanticipated investment opportunity (you cannot always depend on being able to using financing leverage) or a property has some management challenges or lacks appreciation potential.

I am here every day at the office. And although I have a non-compete clause in my independent contractor agreement with each one of my 5 staff members, there is enough work here that my staff can't handle all of it, so I get a lot of overlap. Then from the years of service that I have done, I get referrals from a lot of my former clients. My staff gets first priority on somebody who walks in the door.

Even though I enjoy investing, I still really get a kick out of helping others to invest in real estate too. Sometimes it can be challenging though. I had a client who was a surgeon. At the time, we were doing a lot of build-to-suits. When I built my office building here in this same area, I knew there was property available, and I was working on a committee to attract new medical services to coming here, and I showed them around. I did the orientation when doctors and other medical services people were coming here, and I showed them around our community. I was always open to their needs. My quest was not to sell them anything. My intention was to get them to come here because Del Norte County is so rural and we needed to have good medical services.

So this particular surgeon was interested in this commercial property because it was close to the hospital and it filled her needs. So we built her a 2,300 square foot office with an apartment on top.

She was also a pilot, and I showed her and her husband a house out near the airport. Since she was a general surgeon, and she was on call all the time, she had to have a place here that was convenient to the hospital, as well as a beautiful home to live in when she was off.

They enjoyed that home and the convenience of being so close to the airport. She had her own hangar that was right on the airport; she could literally jump in her plane and taxi out onto the runway and take off!

Eventually, she and her husband were divorced. She moved over to Bend, Oregon. It turns out that she bought and built the office through me at the worst possible time back in '06.

Financially she was totally upside down in the property when the bottom fell out, but I was able to help her; I counseled her not to panic. I leased it to the government as a VA clinic. Interestingly, the VA also leased the upstairs apartment, which was a very nice 950 square foot, one bedroom apartment with a balcony, and they never used it. It was just a huge waste of government funds in my opinion. They ended up leasing it for 5 years and it was very lucrative for her. I sold it for her in 2014, and she made a modest profit. That just goes to show, again, that real estate investing has to be a long term strategy. What she once thought was a horrible mistake, ended up coming out alright. I have to commend the doctor for sticking with it, refusing to take the easy way out and making it work in the end. It took a tremendous amount of integrity to see it through when many others were just walking away.

As they say, "Location, Location, Location"! The principle of Progression and Regression is probably the largest contributing factor to value. You want to purchase the lessor home in the nicer area, so that the other homes can pull your value up.

Secondly, buy what you can afford. Often time's lenders will qualify you for more than you feel comfortable with. Buying a home doesn't have to be the final solution. By using sound principles, and good timing, one can "step-stone" into the home of your dreams. You don't necessarily need to fulfill all of your fantasies right away. It is usually better to work toward that goal.

It seems crazy to me, but I see people work as agents all the time that don't even own any of the commodity they are trying to sell. Here you are, making one of the largest investments you will make in your life and you're choosing to represent you and your best interests, a person who hasn't had the where-with-all to purchase this commodity for themselves. Would you buy a Ford truck from a salesman that drove a Chevy?

Also, work with someone you trust and have a relationship with. Don't just go with the first agent that you meet. Ask questions like:

- How long have you been in the business?
- How many homes have you sold in this neighborhood?
- Have you ever built a home?
- What is your production record?
- How many people are on your staff?
- Do you own your own home?

Tips:

There are many lenders competing out there. The old "Bait-and-Switch" technique is alive and well in the financial institutions industry. Work with a good Real Estate Agent that refers many clients to a Mortgage Broker. That way, the Mortgage Broker will realize that this is not just one client. If anything happens that leaves a bad taste in the mouth of the borrower, it could affect other business in the future.

A good Real Estate Agent is also going to know how to read the financial disclosure estimate that the lender must provide to the prospective borrower. They can ferret out any padding that is common in the industry. For instance, the lender may only charge you 1 point as an origination fee, thereby beating their competitors. However, they may charge then (and systematically, it doesn't matter what they call it-it is still a loan fee that they collect to put in their pockets) an "application fee", "underwriting fee", "verification fee" or a "warehousing fee." All of these fees are nothing more than an additional charge that they attempt to hide in their line items to extract more from you, the borrower. If you have someone representing you that deals with these types of programs every day, they can be a wonderful and powerful service for you to be able to analyze which program is the best fit for you.

Basic home sale recommendations

If a Seller is serious about selling, it is always good to order a Structural Pest Control inspection Report right away. This does a couple of things for a seller. First, it allows the seller time to be able to address some of the issues themselves and save some money (if they have the ability to do so) and secondly, when offering the property, you can then show the clearance certification to a prospective purchaser and assuage any concern about structural defects. A Home Inspection Report is also a good thing to order to address/provide clearance as well.

Homes sell faster when they are staged. If you have to live in the home before escrow is closed, it may be advisable to rent a storage unit and move the clutter to that facility so that the home can be presented in its best possible light. I recommend bread baking in the oven, light symphony music playing, all lights on, curtains opened, weeds pulled, lawns groomed, fresh paint and all deficiencies fixed.

It is always a good idea to perform consistent maintenance to your home. Making sure that the gutters are cleaned out, power-washing the home, painting every 3 years, making sure the grounds are mowed, weeded, fertilized, watered, updating functional obsolescence such as light fixtures, counter-tops, appliances, and so on.

When I was in my first year in the real estate business, I made arrangements to show another agent's home and went over to obtain the key to show the property (I assumed it was going to be vacant since they gave me a key). We parked in the drive-way (I saw no other car), I opened the door and we started in the kitchen, worked through the living room and when I entered the hall and opened the bathroom door-there she was in all of her glory – naked as a "jay-bird!" Rest assured, we now have a policy in place to keep that from ever happening again!

In terms of marketing, in our area the most effective means of promotion is still signage. Over 60% of our leads are generated from our signs. Often, a lead will become a "spin-off" for other showings as well. The next promotional mechanism is posting the listing to our local Multiple Listing Service. From there the listing enjoys a multitude of online sites including, Trulia, Homes.com, Google, Front Door, Propbot, Vast, Hotpads.com, Yahoo, Zillow.com, Oodle, Bobvila.com, Craigslist and Realtor.com, as well as being featured on our own website: investmentrealtyhomes.com.

Why use a Realtor® instead of selling your own home

Most of the time, when a prospective buyer is considering buying a For-Sale-By-Owner property, their immediate thought is that they should be able to garner a substantial discount because the seller is saving money on the Realtor® commission. Secondly, the seller is forced to deal with the prospective buyer directly and in so doing, personalities and therefore egos often get in the way. Additionally, if you are not represented by an independent third party, it is very easy to say something without having time to think it through that may taint your negotiations. If you have an agent, you have time away from the buyer to review everything and you also have their expertise in making a decision. Many potential buyers of owner-offered properties think that they must be "desperate." Moreover, the seller, may or may not, know what the mandatory requirements are for the transfer of a home. Failure to make these required disclosures can be extremely costly. A licensed professional will be familiar with the rapidly changing point of sale requirements and will already have a system in place to make the purchase go smoothly for the buyer.

We are indeed fortunate to serve in an industry that is so resonant, ever-change and constantly on the move. The real estate business is so vibrant that at times one can almost feel a palpable heartbeat.

In addition to this dynamic business that we work in each day, we are blessed to offer our services here in Del Norte County. Tucked away in the extreme North West corner of the state, we have 16 rivers within a day drive (the Smith River is the only undammed river in CA and is a wild and scenic river in our NRA (National Recreation Area). The Pacific Ocean with its rugged coastline and an abundance of sea life is yet another wondrous national feature, and then there is living in the heart of the Coastal Redwood Forest.

The Coastal Redwood is the tallest living organism on the planet. It is quite common for redwood trees to grow in excess of 300 feet. These ancient trees have been on our planet for roughly 240 million years (as compared to modern humans of about 200,000 years). Although, here in Del Norte County, some of our oldest trees are roughly 2,200 years old. These magnificent plants are only found here in Northern CA. Although it is believed their range was much wider in the past, today redwoods are only found growing naturally from Big Sur to Southern Oregon.

If an engineer were to evaluate one of these huge behemoths calculating their massive girth, weight and height, it would be easily determined through well-established engineering tenets that these trees should not be able to stand (the slightest wind should blow them down). They have no "tap root" (a root that goes straight down, thereby stabilizing the portion of the tree protruding above ground) and the relatively small root system that extends approximately 50' from the tree is only 6 to 12 feet deep. How then can these trees survive the floods, winds and storms that they have undoubtedly had to face in their lengthy lives?

Redwoods are a communal tree: they grow in groves, their roots intertwining to for a societal bulwark against what-ever the planet can throw their way. Very much like our native icon, Investment Realty is invested in our community. We survive and derive on strength from the network of relationships we have established and continue to build each day. We work together as a team to provide the optimum in service for people we are blessed to serve.

About the Author

Roy Tedsen
Real Estate Agent/Broker

Investment Realty
1495 Parkway Drive
Crescent City, CA 95531
Office: (707) 464-8757
Fax: (707) 464-1507
Cellular: (707) 218-5202
Email: rtedsen8181@yahoo.com
Website:
www.investmentrealtyhomes.com

Investment Realty offers the full spectrum of real estate needs. From Residential sales to large Commercial projects, we just completed a brand new 10,000 square foot National Retail Outlet Store. Investment Realty is involved both in our local market and in commercial real estate, throughout the Pacific Northwest. Investment Realty was recently well represented at the annual Del Norte Association of Realtors'® Multi-Million Dollar Club Banquet. Our entire staff was honored with awards. Lola Paquette, our Property Manager/Sales received a Million Dollar Club award and Sharon Tedsen, Stuart Nichols, Kevin Hawkins and Roy Tedsen garnered Multi-Million Dollar Club awards. For Roy, this is his 36th Multi-Million Dollar Club award and they are well on their way to fulfilling next year's rigorous requirements.

Investment Realty's success story flies in the face of most of the real estate self-help books that are so popular today. Where others advocate "flipping" properties as soon as possible, and getting by with the minimum possible improvements, we believe in the commodity that we sell. Roy says, "We believe that you 'buy real estate', you don't sell it!" Real estate is an essential ingredient in almost anyone's portfolio and that building equity should be the long term solution to financial success. Real Estate is a long-term investment. It is not meant for quick turnover, instant gratification and market exploitation. The real wealth is in finding properties that have staying power, the right location, built to last and a classic over-all market appeal (rather than trendy, flash-in-the-pan attraction)."

Vincent Lombardi was talking about football when he made his timeless quote: "Winning is not a sometime thing; it's an all the time thing. You don't win once in a while; you don't do things right once in a while; you do them right all the time. Winning is a habit. Unfortunately, so is losing." This same basic premise applies to real estate as well. Why not harness time and money and make it work for you? You're going to have to live somewhere, use that need to catapult you financially into managing an asset-not just having a place to live!

From Beverly Hills/Hollywood to a Career in Real Estate

By Scott Histed

I have been working in real estate for 26 years. I love what I do; it gives me immense satisfaction helping people buy and sell their properties. When I started out, I was selling mostly to people that I knew from LA and then my network in Palm Springs began to grow. I realized that Palm Springs is just such a great small town community, yet there were many things to do and interesting people to know.

My prior experience working in the film business helped me with some of my clients. I've worked with Allison Janney, Ruta Lee, and Lily Tomlin, but I am also equally happy working with a 25-year-old first-time home buyer that just wants to get into the market.

I was working for Neiman Marcus, Paramount and Universal Studios before I became a Realtor®. My work involved event planning for the studios which allowed me to travel to Palm Springs fairly often. One day, I thought to myself, "Perhaps I should just do what I've always wanted to do and just settle in and get my real estate license." So I did. I got my real estate license in 1989 in Los Angeles and then realized there is too much hustle and bustle there. I moved to Palm Springs and never looked back.

I enjoyed my time working with Paramount and Universal. It was a lot of fun because, at the time, the events were completely "over the top." The amount of money they were spending for these events and venues was just completely out of sight. There was no budget and no end to the pocketbook so we had free rein to create the most elaborate and amazing events.

There was one particular time I remember. One night when an executive had a bit too much to drink at a very expensive hotel, all of the furniture ended up in the swimming pool and, of course, my phone started to ring because I was responsible. There were a few events like that that made me decide to change my career. It's funny looking back on it now, but it wasn't as funny then!

Things To Know About Palm Springs

A lot of people say, "Palm Springs is too hot in the summer." Yes, but that is only 8 or 10 weeks of the whole year at most. The rest of the year, we have 42 to 44 weeks that are absolute heaven. So the weather is number one. If you compare to places like Seattle or Detroit where it's cold and rainy and snowy, you might be able to be outside only 10 or 12 weeks a year and the rest you're inside.

Palm Springs is also a fairly small community. There are about 42,000 people in The Coachella Valley, and everybody is laid back and kind. There is a lot of philanthropy here in Palm Springs as well as great architecture and great restaurants. It's the kind of small town that everybody knows everybody else. A lot of people that have second homes here are from Seattle and San Francisco, so there is a lot of diversity here.

When people say Palm Springs, they are often referring to the Coachella Valley. The Valley consists of Rancho Mirage, Palm Desert, Cathedral City, Indio and Indian Wells. However, Palm Springs proper is taking off like wildfire. I actually think I saw Ben Affleck casually riding his bike today. The old Hollywood days are coming back. Most everyone knows about Leonardo DiCaprio purchasing a home here.

Celebrities have enjoyed the escape from Los Angeles to Palm Springs for years and the younger generations are coming back to enjoy the simplicity, yet complicity of the city. Palm Springs has perhaps one of the best art museums in the country. The Palm Springs Art Museum is absolutely phenomenal. We have the McCallum and the Annenberg Theaters as well as many small theaters doing a version of the summer stock theater but in the opposite season. There are many cultural events and approximately 600 Non-Profit organizations here in the Valley. There are many galas and plenty of more casual events to do. You never run out of things to do in Palm Springs.

The Palm Springs Community

I mentioned before that the community is very diverse and has many interesting people. Let me share a great story with you about one of my clients. There was a really nice gentleman that called up and he said, "I've got this house that I inherited and I can sell it now. I inherited it with the caveat that I would not sell it until five feral cats that lived on the property had passed away. The last feral cat has passed away and now I can sell the property." It was a million dollar house and after I sold it he ended up buying a $22,000 mobile home in Cathedral City. He was a really sweet man in his early 70's. He was raised Amish so he didn't really use electricity and didn't want that extravagant house. Even the pool was empty. I can honestly say that he was probably the nicest person I've ever met in my life. Money didn't mean anything to him. In fact, when he inherited the house, he was by himself and wandered into a shop where he read books every day. He didn't have a lot of friends, just a quiet guy that kept to himself. But you would see him out hiking and walking around. But when he left the house, he said, "Do you know of a charity that would like all of the furniture and art because I came here ten years ago with nothing and that's exactly what I'm leaving with; just the sale of the house. You can have all of the contents." So he left everything behind to be given away to charity.

Being involved in the community is very important to me personally and professionally. Just recently, the local paper, "The Desert Sun", named me "Best Realtor®." Every year they do a contest called "Best of the Valley" and they feature different categories such as "Best Bakery", "Best Pizza", and so on. There are about 4,300 Realtors® in the Palm Springs area so I was very flattered to be chosen as Best Realtor®. I'm also a firm believer in continuing education, keeping up on what's new in real estate and financing, and I also do a lot of volunteer work. My partner and I try to support as many charities as possible.

One charity in particular that we support is called Act for MS. Another one is the AIDS Assistance Program which feeds low income men, women, and children that are living with AIDS. FIND Food is another one that we believe in strongly.

Client Representation

When I first meet with a client relate about how I work, we discuss my professional background, my experience and listings that are relevant to their home. I also describe how many listings I'm currently carrying and then we can talk about pricing their home.

A timeline for selling a home keeps everyone on track through the sales process and a calendar of things that will happen; it can include a checklist of work to be done before listing the home, dates for the broker's caravans, open houses, and other parts of the sale before closing.

When I have an initial meeting with a prospective client, some people will say, "Well, I want to see what agents can get me the highest price." However, I recommend to sellers that they decide which agent they like the best, then together we will decide on a price together once they've decided to work with me. You shouldn't choose somebody just because they're telling you, "Oh I can get million dollars for your house." Once a client decides that they're going to work with me, then we will establish a price together that makes sense.

Pricing a home is based on many different factors. First, I'll do a market analysis, and show you all the comps, then we'll price it together. Then, once it's on the market, I do my updates, etc. Once I procure an offer, I work with the seller, line-by-line, and paragraph-by-paragraph making sure they understand everything.

Important steps to complete after an offer are inspections and the many things that go along with inspections. My job is to clearly explain all the different scenarios and options. For example, I might need to point out to the seller that they have 17 days to do their inspection. The Buyer could ask you to repair or something completely out of the blue. In Palm Springs, we have a lot of properties that are built on lease land owned by the Indian Tribes and that can be complicated.

My biggest concern is to always represent my client the best I can. For example: When you have a hot piece of property that gets multiple offers. I worry if I am coaching my client properly, so that they achieve their goals and get what they want. I don't want them to have regrets, as to could have, should have.

When bidding on a house for sale, I will always encourage people to pick the number that they would still feel happy that they got the house but also pick a number that they won't feel like if they didn't bid enough, that they would be upset that they didn't get the house at that price.

There is always vulnerability when I am competing or interviewing for a listing, because usually you are going up against two or three other Realtors®, which are usually friends; there's a limited number of top agents so typically you're competing against your friends or people that you know.

I never speak unkind about another agent. I just say, "The people that you're interviewing are all great and the decision is ultimately yours. You just have to go with who you feel comfortable with." But not everybody behaves like that.

I will illustrate this further. I had a house that I interviewed for the listing and the sellers ultimately interviewed four people. The other three people all knew that Lily Tomlin was my client and the only reason they knew was because I had showed listings that they had, to her. She didn't buy from them. I was the fourth agent to be interviewed and I never mentioned Lily Tomlin's name. About fifteen minutes after I left and got home, my phone rang and the seller said, "We've decided to go with you because you seem to be the most truthful. The other three agents all said that they represented Lily and that if I listed the house with them, they would be able to sell it to her." And he said, "We know this is false because we know that you're friends with Lily Tomlin and we know already that you've been showing her houses. So because you're honest, we're going to list the house with you."

Buying A Home

Here are some tips I recommend to anyone buying a home:

1. Can you afford it?
2. Once you know you can afford it, does the location work for you?
3. How is the condition of the house?
4. How does it fit your lifestyle or your scheme of things?
5. How does it work for you?

Everyone always says, "Location, location, location." Do you have an emotional attachment to this? Could you see yourself calling this Home? Or is this something you're settling for just because there's nothing else?

The reason why I list these questions clearly is that it is frustrating to see someone that can only afford $400,000 or $500,000 for a home and there's nothing but two or three houses available in their price range and they're picking the best of the worst. Oftentimes I've counseled people, "If you don't see what's going to work for you when you first start looking, don't rush. Keep looking." And then after an extended period of looking, if you realize this is what you're going to get for your money, then you have to step back and say, "Well, I'd better make a decision." Instead, the buyer might think about purchasing a condo instead of a house.

Key Point: Buying real estate should never be a rushed decision. It is not like a shirt. You can't return it once you get home because now it is your home.

Financing Your Home

With regards to financing, the most important thing to do is to talk to your CPA. A mortgage broker can certainly tell you what you can afford, but if you have a CPA that you work with you should get their input as well. Consider the following:

- Does it make sense?
- What's a comfortable level?
- What are the tax ramifications?
- Are you selling another house?
- Are you going to owe capital gains on that?

Then, if requested, I generally give my clients the names of multiple mortgage brokers and I suggest that they call them, interview them, and see who they have the best rapport with.

Selling Your Home

There are a few points I would like to cover when selling your home.

First, price it competitively, don't underprice it, don't over-price it, and price it competitively. Here's a good example. There are five houses on a cul-de-sac, all built in the 60's, all identical. The only difference is that they have different elevations and they're painted different colors. One house just sold for $1,400,000. If the other neighbor approached me and said, "What should I do?" I would counsel them to price it at $1,400,000. I wouldn't say underprice it at $1,375,000 so you get multiple offers. I would say, "Price it competitively." If you over price it, the house is going to sit, it's going to get tired, and most buyers don't want to play games. Most buyers want to look at something and say, "Yes, that's priced fairly. I'll buy it."

Secondly, keep it absolutely spotless and have it show-ready 24/7. Palm Springs is a little bit different because visitors come here and want to see houses spur-of-the-moment. If they can't get into them immediately, or if they do get into them and they are not clean and tidy it sets a negative image. So always keep your house super clean and show-ready 24/7.

Next, put yourself in the mind of the buyer. Walk through your front door, start looking at the threshold, look at the weatherstripping around your door. Come inside and look at the baseboards. Are they clean? Is everything meticulous? If it's not, clean it or fix it. Those little impressions make a big, big difference.

Marketing Your Home

My marketing always starts out with a marketing plan. The home absolutely has to be professionally photographed. On the more expensive listings, I actually work with a PR firm that gets the word out. For example, I have a listing right now that's $11,000,000 and the PR firm has sent information to people in Dubai, as well as The Wall Street Journal and The Chicago Tribune. Presenting luxury homes properly requires using PR and of course, high end brochures. When agents print a little brochure off their printer with some hazy photos of a house, that's not professional marketing. People still want something tangible when they walk away from a property. Of course, we are active on social media and networking a property. We are a destination market and people pick up the newspaper or magazine so advertising for events like open houses are essential.

To properly market a house requires an investment of thousands and thousands of dollars. That's what I do because it's what people expect and are entitled to. They want to sell their house. They're banking on me doing the best job possible, so I do whatever it takes to get their home in front of the right buyers.

Increasing The Value of Your Home

The average price of a home that I represent is in the $750,000 range. Some of the simple things that a homeowner can do to increase the value of their home are:

- fresh paint
- new carpeting or flooring
- keeping it show-ready
- keeping it clean, and light and bright

- opening your window blinds

- repairing the obvious things that are broken

- polishing your front door handle

These are simple and obvious things to really detail the house out.

Organizing a home also helps when showing it to buyers. I like to do a walkthrough and make recommendations. Sometimes a client will ask if I can refer them to a professional organizer because buyers will open your drawers and your closets. They might open the kitchen drawer, below the counter where you happen to cut bread all the time, so vacuum up the crumbs. This all helps to get the maximum asking price for the home.

Other factors come into play when reaching the maximum sale price for the home. For instance, proper exposure. As a Realtor®, my job is to educate the seller that they need to respond quickly. If I list a house for $795,000, and the seller says, "I'm not going to go any lower," what happens if we get an offer for $790,000? The seller needs to respond immediately. The seller knows what they'll take or not take, so if the buyer perceives that the seller is playing some sort of game, they'll lose the buyer right away. You've got to be responsive. You've got to be able to expose the house to many potential buyers. And you have to be able to be a good negotiator.

Why Choose a Realtor®

Everyone wants to get the best price for their house and they feel they are justified in asking the price. Choosing a Realtor® helps look at the property objectively because a seller's emotions run high when selling their home. It's very awkward when someone tries to sell their house without a Realtor®. There's also a high degree of transparency required, such as getting information about the disclosures.

Often a buyer will wonder if the seller really knows what they're doing. Have they disclosed everything? Selling a house is not something everybody does every day. Having a professional involved takes the emotion out of it and ensures that things are done right.

I know of a buyer that was looking at a house up in Seattle. And they really wanted a three bedroom house but they could only afford X amount of dollars. A for-sale-by-owner house came on the market with only two bedrooms but it had a very high basement ceiling and they figured they could put two more bedrooms in the basement. The buyers asked the sellers, "Has the basement ever leaked?" "Oh no, we've never had any leakage here," they replied. They bought the house. One day, a man drives by in a truck whose logo said Basement-Be-Dry or something to the effect of a company that waterproofs basements. The driver stops and waves at the owner who was standing on the porch. He gets out of the truck and he says, "Oh, Mrs. Jones, we never heard back from you from that bid we gave you back in December about waterproofing your basement. Did you have a change of mind or are you still interested?" So she played on with it and said, "Let me give you my fax number". Sure enough, the seller knew there was a problem with the basement leaking and he did not disclose it. So the seller, of course, ended up being threatened with, "Either you pay us the $18,000 to waterproof the basement because you lied, or we're going to sue you."

This is why full disclosure is so important in real estate and it's hard to give full disclosure when you're emotionally involved with the sale. Those particular people in my example said, "We still would have bought the house and we would have paid the same price if we had been treated squarely and not lied to."

How to Sell Your Home Quickly

To sell your home quickly a seller needs to cooperate as best as they can, even at times when they don't feel like preparing the house for a showing. Realizing that in this area, sometimes people are only here for a day or two and they're going to buy something. So if you say, "Well, Cousin Sue is coming over...Can they come on Monday?" Typically, I have to explain, "No, they can't come Monday because they're here from LA on the weekend and they're going to buy something this weekend." Be as cooperative as possible with showings. Make sure that if you have pets, there's no sign of pets in the yard or in the house and that it's light and bright.

One thing that a lot of agents are afraid to tell their sellers is, "Please trust me. If you hired me, you must have hired me because you trust me. So please don't micromanage." I've got a seller right now who has never sold a house before. They, of course, think their house is the best of all the other competing houses, which it's actually not. And they want to constantly tell me, "Make sure you bring that umbrella in," and, "When you show it, go over and turn the air conditioning down," and, "Put the pool towels out on the chaise lounges." It's funny (and somewhat frustrating) because I have 26 years of experience doing this. I know exactly what to do. I've been doing this for 26 years. I have to say, "I appreciate your input but you need to let me do my job."

Real estate is demanding but I have found it to be a very rewarding and fulfilling career. I enjoy matching my buyers to the right homes and helping them feel taken care of. Likewise, I also enjoy helping my sellers feel well represented in a fair and honest manner. I look forward to many more years in this rewarding career.

About the Author

Scott Histed

Phone: 760-218-1751
Email: scotthisted@bdhomes.com
Website: www.scotthisted.com

Bennion Deville Homes
Palm Springs Main Office
850 N. Palm Canyon Drive
Palm Springs, CA 92262
Phone: (760) 327-3990
Fax: (760) 327-3991

Originally from a small town near Saginaw, Michigan, I grew up on a small family owned potato farm with 10 brothers and sisters. After spending many years living in Los Angeles I decided in 1989 to venture into Palm Springs and began selling real estate. Since then my appreciation for the Desert and all it has to offer continues to grow.

I offer my clients great negotiating skills, constant communication & updates, comprehensive marketing and a pledge to treat every transaction with the upmost in care & high ethical standards.

Available to both Buyers and Sellers, I look forward to sharing my wealth of knowledge about the Southern California real estate market.

On a personal note, I've got two wonderful golden retrievers that I rescued from the Los Angeles Golden Rescue Club who are my pride and joy. I have a small cabin up in the mountains that I escape to. I also try to do a lot of mid-week getaways to San Diego and places like that. I love to hike and also stay home and do nothing.

Choosing A Real Estate Career

Yashu Toprani

I've been in business all my life. One of the main reasons I became a Realtor® was because I wanted the type of career where I could have flexible hours and be in a position to meet interesting people. I love to meet people and real estate gives me a perfect opportunity to do that.

I came to the United States when I was sixteen years old. Before that I lived in London, England for 10 years. I was born in Nairobi, Kenya. Now I live in Fresno, California with my wife and we are really happy here.

Fresno's one of those cities that's not too small and not too big. It's just the right size. I can go anywhere in Fresno in 30 minutes, one side to the other. I absolutely love that there's practically no traffic compared to L.A. After having lived in L.A., Fresno seems like there's no traffic at all. Commuting in Fresno is only a half an hour a day.

Fresno is also a great city in which to raise a family. One of the things we noticed when we moved from L.A. was how the teenage kids here were very different from the L.A. kids. In a small town, you have more of a family feeling where the kids will actually come and talk to you and don't think that you're too old to talk to them.

Fresno also has a great location in central California. The location makes it easy to get to other areas; it's only two and half hours to San Francisco, two hours to the ocean, two hours to skiing, and two hours to mountains and hiking. We're close to Yosemite, plus we have quick access to many lakes to go boating and fishing.

My Clients

I enjoy the diversity of my client base. Some clients are international and business professionals. Others are physicians who want higher-end homes and investment properties. Locally, I have clients that visit from the Bay Area and Los Angeles who want to invest in Fresno because it's more affordable. Many of my clients that have investment homes rent them out while they are away. With this in mind I refer them to a property management firm that handles all their needs. Focusing on the needs of my clients is what has made me a successful Realtor®.

I have worked hard to grow my business and I get a lot of referrals which I have found is the best way to get new clients. My physician clients are usually referred by either the hospital or one of the offices of the doctor groups. When they hire a new doctor, they refer them to me to find housing.

Over the years, I have done a lot of volunteer work. I was vice-president of a charity called Hearts and Hands for the Handicapped where we collected money for handicapped children in India. I am also past-President of the central California society of India. I have been actively involved for the last fifteen years. I have also been part of the Temple Board and was one of the founding members of the Hindu Temple of Fresno.

Focused on my Customers' Needs

I have always been a customer-focused Realtor®. It is important to recognize what it takes to provide a good customer experience for a buyer or seller. It always starts with listening and understanding their needs.

Before I chose a career in real estate I managed and owned hardware stores and service stations. For a customer to have a good experience they have to feel comfortable in an environment that makes them want to buy. This happens the moment they look at a storefront or a home.

When I managed the hardware store I started up a carpet installation division, then I started manufacturing custom carpets for interior designers. Using my experience of working successfully with interior designers I now work with my clients to showcase their home to sell starting from the outside in.

Buying a Home

When a client wants to buy a home, the first thing to think about is whether the home is in a good and safe location. Consider things like: the school district, the proximity of churches, suitable recreation, and other important amenities.

You must also know exactly what your budget is and what kind of home you can afford. Looking for a home that is outside your budget will not create a positive buying experience. Sometimes people think they can only afford a $200,000 home but they can actually afford a $300,000 home and they short-change themselves by buying a home that is smaller than their needs because they're not sure. Or perhaps they are looking for a $1,000,000 home when they can only afford a $700,000 home. You must know your numbers and be frank with your Realtor® about it.

Regarding financing, I always suggest that a Buyer speaks with their lender before we start looking at homes. If they have good credit, and they know they have good credit, and they're doing conventional 20% financing, I normally advise that they work with a direct lender, for example, Wells Fargo or Bank of America. Typically, my clients receive better rates and lower fees from a direct lender. However, if they have credit issues or no down payment, they've got to go through a mortgage broker, who will help and guide them to the best program they will fit into.

Selling a Home Quickly

When a client approaches me to represent them and sell their home quickly they have to understand that the key point to selling a home quickly is how the home looks. Most people look at the outside of homes at first, so the curb appeal has to be there. You've got to make it look pretty from the outside, even before they walk in.

The next step is to make it inviting inside. When people first walk into the house, it's got to feel inviting. No food odors, no pet odors, and no smoking whatsoever. If there are odors, buyers will think that it's not clean. Those issues will have to be taken care of because that's when buyers initially make the decision. That is a first impression that lasts. In addition, to make the home feel inviting, you must de-clutter and make it look like a model home. Improving the look of the home helps the sale go quickly.

Challenging Deals

Sometimes deals can go sideways, but there is almost always a way to help my clients get what they want. There was a time when we were going through a lot of foreclosures. One of my clients was very interested in a home that was very desirable so we wrote up an offer. In fact, there were multiple offers on the home. The home was listed for $780,000 and we decided to make an offer for $850,000. We don't normally see that in Fresno, where multiple people overbid on a home, but this was a one of a kind home and my client loved it. Our offer was accepted, but when we went to the appraisal, the appraisal came at $750,000. We were $100,000 off. This was a foreclosure so it was owned by the bank. At this point we had to strategize and think about what the bank was likely to do. We took a leap of faith and requested the bank to take $100,000 less - and they accepted it! My client ended up getting that dream home for $750,000 even though they had offered $850,000. The unique part of the transaction was not only was the house very special but it was also well cared for despite being a foreclosure. The property is located high up on a hill and it has a million dollar view in the back. The back yard is perched on a cliff and it has a gorgeous infinity pool. The home was built by a custom builder who had done a lot of high end touches and extra custom work, such as a circular staircase inside as you walk in. The kitchen was really well done and the flooring was unique too. In addition, the home had a huge balcony off the back so the owner could really entertain. This is an excellent example of why it is important to show a home in the very best state it can be. This way you can generate a lot of interest and in this case have multiple offers on the same property.

Marketing

Marketing a home is a complex process that involves different techniques using print, social media and video. We advertise our listings on Facebook. We also advertise in industry publications, such as the Home magazine as well as newspapers. Our goal is to make it easy for buyers to contact us. To that end, we use a 1-800-number on each sign so they can call right when they're driving by a home. This way, they can get immediate information if they're interested in knowing more about the home. They get a recorded message with some details about the home, and we get the phone number of the client so we can call them back and follow up. We use the same principle with people that don't want to make a phone call. In that case we use a text message system. We also have virtual tours set up online for our clients. We syndicate to all major portals like Realty.com, Zillow, Trulia, and about 120 other websites. We also advertise on Craigslist and of course, we do a YouTube video as well.

Marketing is a very dynamic part of the sales process. We have standards that help us maintain consistent success for our clients. Good photography is key to showcase the home as a product. I always use professional photographers to take high end photographs. Plus, we have a system where we get feedback from agents that have shown it. The clients also get access to that. We send out three emails to the agents that have shown it and if they have any feedback, the homeowner can see it.

Providing feedback to the seller closes the information loop from agents that have shown the home. This helps maintain momentum during the sales process and provides a real-time assessment of the home's market value. This also helps increase the seller's confidence in our marketing skills. Typically, we have open houses on a Wednesday or a Thursday for agents and brokers. And we provide lunch for them - Realtors® love food!

Showing the Home

Once you get sellers and buyers talking they always focus on price so it's important to show the home in the very best circumstances to justify the price of the home. A seller will want the best price they can get. To help arrive at the highest number we have a report that we go through. It's called the Maximum Home Value Audit, where we analyze the home for anything that needs to be changed.

To ensure that we are thorough, we go through each section of the home and systematically look at each room to see what we can do to maximize the price. Either it needs new paint, new carpet, or sometimes it's just a simple thing like dressing it up or taking down curtains. A lot of times we see people with curtains and it makes the house look and feel darker. I know that's a personal preference. But oftentimes, where you don't need the privacy, if trees are growing in the backyard, removing the curtains lightens the house. Sometimes I recommend people do cosmetic changes in the home, such as switching tile counters to granite if they can afford it. Often it's small changes that will make an increase the sale price.

We also provide a free staging consultation to all our clients. A professional home stager walks through the house with them and suggests to the client what they need to do.

When showing the home, basic things need to be taken care of, such as keeping it clean and decluttered, picking up and organizing the kids' toys, and a perfectly clean and tidy kitchen. Also, make sure it's bright by turning on all the lights.

Weather makes a big difference for a listing as well. When you're showing a home in summertime in Fresno you must have the AC on. Potential buyers will be uncomfortable if it's not on. If they are hot and uncomfortable, they will get a bad impression of the overall house because they'll just be thinking, It's hot in here. It's hot in here. But if the room is kept cool and inviting, they will focus on the home.

How to Choose a Realtor®

Whether a client is a buyer or a seller they all want the best level of service they can get. It's important that when they are interviewing an agent or a broker they should ask relevant questions, such as:

- How long the listing will stay on the market?

- What kind of price do you think we can get?

This can protect the client from agents that just want come in and take a listing and will say whatever the client wants to hear.

For example, some agents will tell the homeowner that they can get $650,000 when they know real value of the home is more like $600,000. The homeowner lists with them and it sits on the market for months and all it does is disappoint the homeowner. The agent tries to make it work by reducing the price to $600,000 two months later, but in the meantime, the homeowner is the one who suffers. To that extent, we firmly believe in pricing the home correctly in the market to make it sell quickly. When someone's selling, they want to get it done quickly and move on. That's why they put it on the market. They don't want to be hanging around there for six months or eight months. It costs them money, stress and sometimes, heartache.

Another effective way to screen a prospective agent is to ask them how fast their listings sell. Our firm has a one day listing agreement. So if you don't like us, fire us. Basically, we don't want you to be tied to us for six months if it's not working. We know you're going to like us – and if for whatever reason you don't, just let us know and in 24 hours we will cancel your listing agreement, remove the signs and you'll be free to go do whatever you need to do. This gives us marketplace credibility and maintains transparency and honesty through the sales process.

It's critical to manage expectations in real estate because the stakes are high and clients do not want to be disappointed. A real estate agent should be very straightforward with the client and give them information that's going to work in the market. When you're a buyer, you want to know that what you're buying is the right home for you. The agent should be able to guide you. For example:

- Where is the right home located?

- Is it the right home for you?

- Or if it's over-priced or under-priced, what kind of offer you should make on a home?

Your real estate agent should be there to help you honestly, not just to say yes and be agreeable. Many times I've told people not to buy a home, even if they like it, but if it backs up to a major cross-street it will sell a lot slower because of the street noise in the back. When it comes time to resell the home, the problem resurfaces because when you try to sell a home in a difficult location, you're going to have a hard time selling it. This means you're going to have to discount it. Unless you really love that home, there's really no reason to buy it.

Buyers should always keep resale in mind when they purchase a home. We sell our homes when we are motivated to sell. Job situations can change suddenly, and in a moment's notice you've got to move and sell your home. I tell my clients to always look and see how easy will the home be to sell if you need to sell it for whatever reason. So when you're motivated to sell your home quickly it needs to be ready for a showing at any moment. This means that the home needs to be properly maintained throughout the years.

Communication

Realtors® sometimes need to have difficult conversations with clients when they are going through life changes. Good communication skills are crucial to being a successful Realtor®. Typically, if my clients are buyers who are actively looking in the market, then I'll meet with them once a week at least. Sometimes if they are not nearby, they'll start looking early on. The Internet enables many of our clients to start looking at homes six, eight, or ten months before they are ready to buy. Many clients do their market research before meeting with me. So if they're browsing through Trulia they can look up a listing agent's information and they can call for more information on that house. I try to touch base with long distance buyers every four to six weeks, depending on how the whole search is going.

Why I Love Real Estate

I've sold million-dollar homes and I've sold to folks buying their first home for $150,000. One thing that I've found is that my biggest joy has been seeing the first time home buyer buy their home. It's just so exciting to see them get their dream home and move into it. It's the first step in home ownership that they've had and to see how happy they are, that just brings a big smile to my face. I'm honored to be a part of that event in their life. That's always an exciting time for everyone involved. To celebrate, I usually give them a gift, something personal to their tastes or lifestyle. I try to personalize it to each client.

I am so happy that I chose real estate as a career because I truly enjoy helping people navigate through all the steps of a real estate transaction. If I can take away their stress and make it easier for them, then I feel that I am serving them well.

About the Author

Yashu Toprani

Rod Aluisi Real Estate
1170 E Champlain Dr #109,
Fresno CA – 93722

Office Phone: 559-549-8569
Cell Phone: 559-512-1148
Email: yashut@gmail.com

Yashu Toprani started his career at age seventeen, working at a hardware store. He quickly worked his way up and became the manager at age 20. From there, he developed a carpet installation division, which eventually developed into manufacturing custom carpets for interior designers. It was through his work with interior designers that Yashu became interested in the real estate field.

Yahsu is a full time real estate agent. His philosophy about real estate is that he is there to help two parties (buyer and seller) find each other and complete a transaction with a minimum of fuss and headache. He believes that the real estate agent should not stand in the way.

Yashu is an advocate for his clients. His job is to obtain the best price, terms and conditions for his client, not to worry about the other parties' preferences or feelings. He finds that real estate transactions are far more satisfying to both parties when the closing is a pleasant experience for everyone.

Why I Enjoy Making Real Estate As Easy As Possible For My Clients

Quincy Virgilio

I decided on a career in real estate because I was looking for a way to provide for my family that was less stressful that what I was currently doing. Prior to real estate, I was the owner of 5 pizza parlors, which I started with my brother right out of school. It was back-breaking, unrewarding, and unfulfilling work. It was not fun. I did not enjoy the grind of having to do that kind of work on a daily basis; being in my pizza parlors every day, working with 190 employees, most of them teenagers who often did not show up for work.

I was very interested in looking at a career where I could not only serve people in my community, but serve my family as well and have an unlimited potential for expanding myself as a person. I was 35 years old and at that time, I had two children - a 12 year old and a 10 year old.

I had a customer by the name of Gail Christiansen who used to come in and talk to me about what he did for a living as a real estate broker and mortgage broker. He told me he felt I was a very personable guy and I could do well in a business where I was dealing with people; a business where they were doing multiple hundred thousand dollar transactions, instead of ten dollar transactions like I was doing then. He made it sound very appealing.

So I left my pizza business in my brother's care, and got my real estate license and went to work for Gail. I worked for him for two years and, in that two years, I was able to successfully obtain my broker's license and then open my own business.

Santa Clara County

Santa Clara County is a huge community with two million people and many sub-cities. I have lived here for 51 years and work in all parts of the county. The whole world knows Silicon Valley and it started right here in San Jose, which is the town I live in.

San Jose is a huge city. It is the tenth largest city in the United States with a population of 1.1 million people. It is ethnically diverse, and has many diverse industries as well. There is a lot of tech, biotech and manufacturing companies. We have all kinds of great city life: arts and crafts, bars, restaurants, and parks. It is a great place to live. We are 25 minutes from Santa Cruz, which is right on the coast, an hour and twenty minutes from Monterey, an hour from San Francisco, and four hours from Lake Tahoe if you want to go to the snow.

Follow The Education

My specialty is helping sellers. I prefer to be more of a listing agent than a buyer's agent. Of course I do work with buyers too; most of the buyers I work with are people who have been referred to me, or they are past clients where I am selling their home and they are buying another home. However, the majority of my business is focused on listing and selling.

I like listing and selling because listings control the market. As an example, in our area at the time of this writing, there currently 1000 listings and there are 13,000 Realtors®. So, if I have a listing, I have one client to worry about: my seller. Six, seven, eight or ten buyer's agents will have to be out there looking for my home. I deal with one client and I get to select, with the help of the seller, the agent we are going to work with. We have the product, so all the buyers come to us, as opposed to being a position of the buyer going to the product.

When someone is looking for a real estate agent, they should look at how much education they have, because it shows two things. It shows dedication to the profession – that they are always trying to improve to ensure they are on top of what is going on in the industry – and it shows they care about their industry. As a client, you want to know that your Realtor® is on top of what they are doing by the education they have and the certifications they have earned. It is like having a Master's degree in real estate; additional education is required to obtain a broker's license and these certifications. It is a higher level of education in the industry.

My designations are:

• CRS is a Certified Residential Specialist - you earn this by taking more classes and it is also based on production. You have to have a minimum production to become a CRS. It is a designation that is from the National Association of REALTORS® (NAR). I would estimate that only 3% of all REALTORS® in the United States have the designation of CRS.

• GRI is Graduate of the Realtor® Institute - another NAR education program. You earn this by taking a twelve course program. This program helps you understand how to sell and interpret the marketplace.

• SRES is a Seniors Real Estate Specialist – this designation means I am qualified to address the needs of home buyers and sellers aged 50+ and help them through the major financial and lifestyle transitions that occur when buying, selling and relocating.

• CDPE is a Certified Distressed Property Expert® - this is the nation's fastest growing independent real estate designation. A CDPE has a thorough understanding and knowledge of foreclosure avoidance options available to homeowners. CDPEs can provide solutions, specifically short sales, for homeowners facing market hardships.

- CPRES is a Certified Probate Real Estate Specialist – a Certified Probate Real Estate Specialist has been specially trained by US Probate Services on the process of selling real estate through the probate process. A CPRES Realtor® understands the unique complications, the time-sensitive process, and adheres to the best practices necessary to navigate the potentially treacherous transaction to completion and help the estate realize a win-win transaction.

Further, I am a top producer with Keller-Williams, and I sell between 25 and 30 homes annually. 74% of the people in our marketplace sell 4 or less homes per year. I am in the top 5%.

Community Work

I am very involved in organized real estate. I served as president of the Santa Clara County Association of Realtors® in 2009 - coming from directors of the Santa Clara Association of Realtors®, treasurer and president-elect, and then president. I also currently serve as chairman of the board for our multiple listing service - MLS Listings - which services 16,000 Realtors® in five counties. MLS Listings is a regional multiple listing service. I am also a commissioner for the Housing and Community Development Commission for the city of San Jose. I also served for four years as a director for the Silicon Valley Housing Trust, which is an affordable housing program. I now serve as a director for the Fairgrounds Management Corporation. Santa Clara County Fairgrounds is a 110 acre parcel that is managed by the county. It is about to be redeveloped, and that is why I am on it. The annual fair has shrunk considerably; when I was a kid it was a huge ten day fair. Now it is down to three days and is very small. The entire 110 acres is going to be redeveloped. It will have a community center, a small piece of the fairgrounds will stay, and likely some affordable housing.

I support several charities. St Jude has always been one of my favorites because of the work they do with children. I used to have my own bicycle ride that was called "Pedaling for Possibilities." People would sponsor you for every mile you rode. We would take that money and donate it to the Community Family Services which helps single mothers with childcare. "Pedaling for Possibilities" lasted for six years.

Buying and Selling

When you are buying a home, the first thing you need to think about is affordability. It is important to meet with a mortgage banker, mortgage broker, or lender of some sort to understand the finances and costs of owning a home. This goes beyond a mortgage.

The next thing you want to know about is the neighborhood. Look at the statistical data about crime, the schools, and generally what kind of community it is.

You also need to look at the value of property. Make sure the homes in the neighborhood are appreciating. Make sure if you do things to improve the house you would not out-price the neighborhood. And make sure it is a neighborhood you feel comfortable in – this is the most important thing.

Before I came to work at Keller-Williams, I owned a real estate company and mortgage company. I was a mortgage broker from 1998 to 2009. I owned two different companies: The Mortgage Network and California Property Network. One sold real estate, one generated mortgages.

When I meet with people about financing, I talk about the importance of having their financing options organized before they start looking for a home, that they have been pre-approved for a mortgage by a reputable mortgage broker or banker, and the importance of making sure the mortgage person can perform in a timely fashion so no contingency timelines are missed and they can close on time. You also want to have a mortgage person who is truthful and speaks to you in a direct and almost forceful manner. People need to be directed in this area. People need to understand the importance of the financing and the documentation the lender needs. They need to understand the importance of having it there in a timely manner. Sometimes that takes a mortgage person being direct to accomplish this.

I am not a fan of someone obtaining a mortgage online. It is hard to have accountability with someone on a website. It is about relationships. You want to have a relationship with your mortgage banker or broker. You need someone to whom you can ask questions, who is there for you, who guides you through the process, and who can be held accountable.

A good mortgage person will clearly explain to the buyer what sort of things can make a deal fall through. Sometimes it comes down to the mortgage person telling the clients not to go out and buy a car. Do not open new credit card accounts. These are things that are so important to have done up front. It has happened in the past where someone went out and bought a car in the middle of a transaction and it would have prevented them from buying their house.

We have learned to warn our clients about these things going into the transaction so nothing can go wrong. Most of the issues have to do with timing of transactions.

Tips On Selling Your Home

If a homeowner wants to sell their home quickly, one of the top things they should do is price it properly. The market will tell you what the value of your home is and the market is never wrong. What I mean is that the sold properties like yours will be a very good guideline for what your home is going to sell for. Everyone has an idea of the value of their home. If you think, "My house is worth a million dollars," but your neighbor sold theirs for $850,000, the reality is that the market has shown and proven the neighborhood is worth $850,000.

The second task is to prepare your home for sale. You need to de-clutter and remove a lot of stuff from the house. Then you need to do any touch-ups that can be done to make the home show better - so when someone walks in, there is a wow factor. I help my clients with this and I do whatever it takes. I have some clients who are older and cannot do these things, so I have a list of service providers that can help prepare a home for sale.

I have had several instances when an elderly client had to go to a nursing home. Often, these people have a collection of items in their home and it is very cluttered and full of stuff: magazines, records, furniture, glassware, and collectibles. I recall one particular client had closets full of hats! I have a great company that actually comes in and goes through and tries to do two things - either sell the items through a garage sale or donate the things the family does not want. I have another service that can actually pack, move and store whatever needs to be done to get the stuff out of the property.

I did have a listing once that had a garage full of garbage. It was horrible. It was a couple who were going through a divorce and the woman had some mental health issues. She lived in the house with two of her children for about three years. In the last year, she had simply stopped taking out the trash. Every week, she would place the trash in the garage. For a whole year! The stench was unbearable. Luckily, I have a great company that has a big dump truck and workers who came in and shoveled all the garbage into the dump truck and took it to the dump. Then we went through the process of cleaning out the garage and decontaminating it. That was a big job but she clearly needed help and that's part of what I do.

In an effort to make things as easy as possible for my clients, we also help people move furniture and take things out of the house. It is all part of my service, to make sure the house shows properly and is put in the best light possible. I have an assistant and anything I need, she is there for me. I have also had my family help - whatever it takes.

We have become so organized; we have checkpoints along the way to make sure we do our job so nothing goes wrong. We are proactive to make sure all timelines are met, all paperwork is properly taken care of, all service providers are doing their job, and the buyer's agent is doing his job. We are at the point now that we do not come up against something too unusual that the deal wouldn't close.

Selling Your Home

I think Open Houses are a great idea, but not all Realtors® do. In our marketplace, it is typically one weekend of open houses and then the house is sold right after. Going back a few years, there were times when open houses were held for three months going before you found a buyer. We like to make some of our open houses special. We are trying to incorporate a Friday night open house for neighbors with a little wine and cheese. This will eliminate the neighbors on the weekends. I invite the neighbors over and get to talk with them about what is going on in the neighborhood. If it is a town home or a condominium complex, "How's the homeowners association? Is there anything we should know? Anything weird been going on in here? When are the Halloween parties? Do you guys have a parade or anything?"

We make it easier and smoother for our clients by handling all the details of the transaction. We want to be the person who handles, for example, the inspections. We order and schedule the inspections ourselves. We make sure we can provide the service providers that can do any needed repairs or improvements to the property. If we need to paint, we organize it - we get the painter to give the bid, and do the job. If there is any termite work needing to be done, we make sure that we are coordinating this for the client. The client should only be aware of what is going on and not having to do anything.

When we want to stage the house, we bring someone in who can help by telling them, "Move this, move that, move this, we are going to change this around." We handle all of this for the seller. We are not going to have them go out and find the service provider to do these things.

We understand that we make a good amount of money for what we do. So we want to ensure that our clients don't have to do anything other than be ready for when the contract comes in. They need to fully understand the contract - which is what we educate them on - and be able to accept or counter an offer.

Don't try to sell your home yourself

There are many reasons why someone should hire a Realtor® and not try to sell the home by themselves. The first reason is the impression when you see a sign that says "For Sale By Owner." You will have strangers knocking on your door and you do not know who they are, if they are qualified, or if they have the capacity to buy your home. Usually, if they are represented by someone, there's a good chances they've been qualified.

The reason you should hire an agent is because he or she can maximize the exposure of your property. In my marketplace, there are 13,000 Realtors® in Santa Clara County who are going to know your property is for sale and might have a buyer for it. As opposed to a Craigslist ad, or an ad in a newspaper, or a sign on your front lawn that says "For Sale By Owner," I am going to maximize what you get for your property. I will probably get you a higher dollar amount, so even after you pay my commission, you will walk with more money.

There is a legal liability that needs to be taken into consideration when you are selling your home on your own. There are statutory forms that are required by law. The Transfer Disclosure Statement that we use to sell a house is required by law. Every person who transfers a property has to complete one.

Most importantly, I am here to protect you. That's my job. With all the disclosure paperwork that needs to be done, I am liable for four years on the sale of your home for everything we have done. You are going to be protected and no one is going to come back to you and say, "Hey, you did not do ABC." It is a big responsibility and one that I am confident undertaking because of all the years of experience and education I've had.

It's All In The Process

After a seller has agreed to work with me, I rely on my assistant to ensure the administrative tasks are taken care of. She coordinates all service providers and all the activities. The first thing we do is a home inspection, pest inspection, roof inspection, and a chimney inspection. The reason we do these things up front is because we want to make sure we know everything there is to know about the property. There cannot be a surprise when the buyer does their own inspections. If you do not do the pre-inspections and a buyer finds something wrong, they can come back and try to renegotiate the price or even cancel the transaction because of the issues that were found. We do not want to be in that position.

The next step is preparing the home for sale. We assist in the guidance of de-cluttering and we follow up to make sure it is done. We bring in any service providers we may need for painting, staging, decorative issues, or repairs. When we have done all the clean up, and made sure the house is de-cluttered, painted and repaired if necessary, and it has been staged, then we bring in our photographer who does our entire photography package. He takes the pictures, creates the video, our marketing pieces, the print pieces, and all our online posting of that information.

Then we schedule our first open house. Typically, we will try to get a property on the market on a Tuesday. Then we have a broker tour on Wednesday or Thursday, where brokers come through the property from their marketing meetings. The following weekend we have an open house where we look for all the thousands of people who want to buy the home.

Our marketing also includes the complete social media package. We do a "Just Listed" email blast to my database. I keep track of other agents who sell homes in different neighborhoods, so we send an email such as: "We have a listing in that neighborhood; you had a buyer that once bought a property there. Do you have another buyer for that neighborhood?"

The process for closing the deal, of course, is more complicated than just closing a deal. We usually have an offer period, because our market is so hot right now. We set an offer date and then we review the offers with the seller, do an analysis of each offer, go through a counter-offer process if necessary, or accept the best offer. Then, of course, hold everyone to the terms of the offer. That means timelines, contingency removals, if they are having an inspection period of their own, then the funding of the property's loan and, of course, the recording of the deed and closing.

The best thing a seller can do to facilitate a smooth quick sale and still get the price they want for their home is be invisible for the process. When agents are showing the home, I do not want my owners there. When we are having an open house, I do not want my owners there. I do not want them doing the tour, telling everyone, "This is what we did here and there." That information is something we should learn from them and showcase in our marketing package. In order to do this, I need them to be out of the way for a little bit, until it is important for them to be there, which is when the offers come in.

I communicate with the sellers on a regular basis. I make sure they know what is going on, such as how many people came through during the open house, the feedback we received, and what traffic we are getting on our website. They will know what is going on but they also have to "let go and let be."

In this marketplace, I communicate right after the open house. If we are on the market for longer than that, I communicate with them on a Monday or Tuesday of each week. Right now, it is moving so quickly that I communicate daily.

I currently have three listings that keep me busy. Over the next 5-10 years I want to grow my business to be more of a team-oriented business, where I have a buyer's agent, someone that is a listing specialist, and I am more of a communicator with the clients. My assistant does a lot of that now, but I want to grow it to a higher level. I am always looking for more business and a way to do it in more efficient ways.

About the Author

Quincy A. Virgilio, Jr.

Phone: 408-583-3733
Mobile: 408-832-2912
Fax: 408-273-6833

Email: quincy@qavirgilio.com

Office:
Keller Williams
San Jose - Silicon Valley
2110 S. Bascom Avenue, Suite 101
Campbell, CA 95008

Quincy Virgilio has 22 years of experience helping Buyers and Sellers achieve their goals.

His background includes Mortgage Finance, which helps all his clients understand the financial aspects of buying and selling a home.

He serves his clients' needs and he is dedicated to their success. He is actively involved in his profession, and he has served as the Chairman of the Board for his Regional MLS, The President of our Local Realtor® Association and currently serves as a Director for the National Association of Realtors®, and as a Director for the California Association of Realtors®.

I Built My Career by Helping Families

By Tony Ayon

While working as a program coordinator, developing economic and educational programs for people living in affordable housing, I started my career in real estate. Before that, I never really thought about a career in real estate. The only experience I had in real estate was when I purchased my first home at age 23. Nonetheless, I studied to get my real estate license, took my test, and passed! There I was with a real estate license and no idea what to do.

One day, while networking at a home show in Bakersfield I ran into some friends who were working as lenders and they introduced me to an agent in town. The agent and I started talking and she said, "Why don't you work as my assistant?" I did, and as time went by I got better at the business and started to build my clientele. Here I am 15 years later, still at it.

I loved developing economic and educational programs for families. I did not realize it then, but helping families is what drives me. In real estate, I am still helping families but in a different capacity; I am helping them make the biggest purchase of their lives. I especially enjoy helping people who never thought they would own a home. Seeing the joy when I hand them the keys to their new home is a great experience. They are so grateful and all of a sudden I am part of the family. This is why I love real estate so much and why this career has worked out so well for me.

About Bakersfield

Bakersfield is a unique place. Many people say it's too hot, and it's true that we do have about 10 - 15 days a year where it gets to be over 100 degrees. I think it's worth it because we are literally an hour and thirty minutes away from one of the largest cities in the world - Los Angeles. We are 90 minutes from the beach, 35 minutes from the mountains, and 30-40 minutes from the actual desert. When you live in Bakersfield you have access to all of this. You can drive there for the day and return home, where cost of living is affordable.

In Bakersfield, you can actually afford to live in a nice house and still be able to do other things like take a vacation - you are not just working to own a home. The median house price, as we speak, is $219,000 – so the bottom line is that people can afford to live here. We have good, honest, hardworking people who live in this city and Kern County. Generations of families have grown up here.

Economically, Bakersfield consists of a lot of oil, agriculture, and manufacturing industries. It is very community oriented; even though it is a big city with over 350,000 people, it has a small town feel to it. We have great restaurants, great parks and recreation, and we are very giving. For example, the Bakersfield Relay for Life event in 2015 raised over $1,000,000. That is the beauty of this city.

Community Involvement

Interestingly, I am the first male president in the Bakersfield network of the Women's Council of Realtors. We also started a non-profit organization called Real Estate Professionals Family Relief Fund. In our industry, there are a lot of people who do not have medical insurance. Tragedies happen all the time, so we raise funds for these instances. We help our own industry and it is all inclusive: escrow and title, home inspectors, Realtors®; anyone in the real estate industry can apply for funds if they are in need. It is one of the things I am very passionate about, giving back to the real estate community. I am also a big supporter of the American Heart Association. We participate in the annual Bakersfield Heart Walk and raise an average of $5,000 a year for the Heart Association.

I have been involved in different community organizations for a long time. I believe it is the giving part that actually helps our business. Currently, I am in a position where I donate and help raise funds for different things. I am around people who have the same passion as me. I build relationships with these people. Eventually people are going to buy a home - guess who they are going to call? When you are involved in, and give back to, your community, your community will give back to you. You are a part of the community; they trust and believe you because you are sitting in the same room with the same goal of helping others.

I also support a boxing program that helps kids and I support those programs for people who live in affordable housing and low income housing. I sit on Boards with people who buy and sell property. If you give to your community, your community is going to give back 100% more than you give.

Education Mitigates Mistakes

In my second year in real estate when I really started getting busy, I was helping a buyer and I made a terrible mistake. My mistake cost this buyer his deposit which was $1,000. I recognized that $1,000 is a lot of money for someone who is buying an $80,000 home. I told myself that would never happen again. I made him a promise that if he ever trusted me to help him buy a home again, I would more than make up for my $1,000 mistake. Twelve years later, he called me and asked me to help him. At the end of the transaction, I gave him all of my commission to make up for what I lost when I could not afford to give him that kind of money. When it happened, I remember telling myself, I am going to go out and get educated so this will never happen again. It was a mistake I made because I did not know any better.

I made it a point to get my Broker license, Graduate Real Estate Institute (GRI) designation and my Certified Real Estate Specialist (CRS) designation. Education is very important. I have quite a few other designations: CDPE, SFR, RCC, and CNCS . I have these designations because I thrive on learning more about my profession so I can be the best agent for my clients. Achieving my GRI took an entire year of monthly classes, 8 hours a day. My CRS was another grueling and expensive designation I achieved. Those two designations gave me the knowledge and education I needed. I can now pass this knowledge on to other agents as we work together. I am a big believer in education, period, but when you become a Realtor®, you need to be educated in your craft. Just like doctors; they get their license but also obtain further education. I believe that as Realtors®, we should do the same.

Choosing a Realtor®

When you are looking for a Realtor®, ask a friend who they used. The goal, as a Realtor®, is to give each client the best experience. If that was accomplished, your job is done.

The next step as a consumer – whether buying or selling a home – is to educate yourself. There are so many places online where one can go to do research on what some of the real estate verbiage means. Also, ask your Realtor® for information. Do not be afraid to ask questions! There are no stupid questions. You are making a big purchase, or selling a big dollar item, so you have to feel assured and comfortable with what you are doing.

My third recommendation is that if you have a feeling that the Realtor® you've chosen is not a good match, walk away. You do not owe anything to anyone. If you do not feel comfortable, the chemistry is not there, or you feel you are not being treated the way you deserve walk away. There are a lot of really great Realtors® out there. It goes back to what I was saying earlier about relationships. The relationship with your Realtor® is built right away; you know when it's a right fit, you feel it.

Local Financing

The financing part of real estate is another situation where people need to do their homework. One of the biggest, and not too popular, suggestions I give is to try to find someone in the local market. When you search the internet or big banks, they give you special rates, but you are dealing with someone out of state. There is no opportunity to do the face-to-face meeting. It is very hard for us

Realtors® when an issue comes up. If they're out of town, I can't walk into their office and say, "Hey, what is going on with my buyer's deal?" and deal with it in person. It usually consists of phone calls and what if they don't answer the phone?

That's why I always say, find someone local. There are very good local lenders in Bakersfield. Once again, ask your friends and family who they used.

Selling Your Home Fast

When it comes to selling your home fast, the best advice I can give is to listen to what your Realtor® is telling you. Look at the comparables. If you price a property too high, it will sit on the market. If you price it a little lower, you might get more interest; more people coming through your property.

If you want a quick sale, there are some quick and easy recommendations that will make your property look nice without costing you a lot of money. For example, flowers, painting, and de-cluttering will make the home appear open and inviting. When it comes to selling your property fast because you want to move, then you have to pay attention to where the market is and try to be at market or a little below market so you can get as many people in the door as possible. Hopefully, you will get the price you want with a quick turnaround.

You might end up with multiple offers as well as multiple opportunities such as different types of financing; cash, conventional, or FHA. You can pick which one works best for you. Your Realtor® will help guide you through this process.

Experience Leads to Creativity

I had a situation where my team was representing a buyer, and the seller failed to disclose there was a septic tank on the property. In the eleventh hour, it was brought to our attention, via the appraisal, so the lender required a certification. Someone had to pay for that certification so we had to figure it out. The seller couldn't pay for it; they were just breaking even with the sale. The buyer obviously did not want to pay for the certification because they did not feel it was their responsibility. At the end of the day, we were able to get the seller credit through the lender which gave them a little extra money to pay for the certification, so it all worked out.

You never know what will happen when you show properties. I remember one time when a fellow Realtor® and I went to show a vacant property to a potential buyer. We walked through the vacant house and everything appeared okay. We walked into the back yard and were looking around when all of a sudden we heard a sound, "cling cling, cling cling". I thought, "What is that noise?" Suddenly, a pit-bull is running full speed at us! The other Realtor® and I ran inside the house and - I am embarrassed to say – we totally forgot about the buyers. We ran in the house, closed the door, and then thought, "Oh no! The buyers!" We yelled, "Get in here, there's a dog coming!" We barely got them inside the house and closed the sliding glass door before the dog reached us. Luckily, the pit-bull was just running over to greet us. When he got to the glass door and saw us, he just licked the glass. He was not trying to attack anyone. Apparently, the neighbor's fence was broken and his dog thought he'd join us for a friendly visit.

Hard Work Pays Off

The first four years I was in real estate, I never took a vacation. I worked seven days a week and was able to build a referral base from working so much. On the weekends, I went to the swap meet and put houses on pin-up boards. People at the swap meet would come through and I would show them the listings and take their information. I would then qualify them throughout the week and show them the property. On the weekend, I would go to the swap meet again with a whole new set of houses. Then it got to the point where people went to the swap meet to find me because they wanted my help to either buy or sell a home. After that, I was able to build such a good referral base I did not have to go to the swap meet anymore. All my business is referral based now. Four years of hard work and no vacations paid off.

I still work listings because I take care of my personal referrals. One of the things my agents appreciate about me is that I am in the trenches with them. I work just as hard as they do; I have listings, buyers, and I show properties. I thoroughly enjoy working with people and helping them buy and sell their homes.

The Importance of Marketing

When I have a listing, I advertise in great magazines and on my company web pages. I am a big Facebook believer, so I always put each of my listings on Facebook to let people know what's coming. I also share it with all the agents within the company. I think when I meet with a potential client for a listing presentation, 99.9% of the time I already have the listing. It's just how I market, because, as I said, my business is all referral based. I let them know what I am going to do: magazine advertising, newspaper advertising, signs, flyer boxes, word of mouth, and then social media. I can't tell you how many sales I've had because of Facebook.

I also hire a professional photographer to take pictures of my listings so my listing presentation is very nice. As I am leaving, I take a picture of the front of the house and post it on Facebook saying, "Coming on the market tomorrow. This southwest home has three bedrooms, two baths, with a pool, $280,000. Contact me for details" before it even goes on the market. This is a big advantage to the seller, because the seller knows I am working for them and I am being proactive in getting their property sold as quickly as possible.

Using a Realtor®: Statistics Do Not Lie

Statistics show there is a better chance you will sell your home for more money if you use a Realtor® rather than if you do not. The number one reason is exposure. You are able to expose your home to a broader base of potential buyers, bringing potential bidding wars, more offers, and more opportunities.

Most people who opt to sell their home on their own – referred to as a For Sale by Owner - don't realize all the disclosures and protections that are required to sell a property. They have to submit certain documentation to the buyer regardless of whether they listed with a real estate company or not. By using a Realtor®, you know the correct forms are being submitted on your behalf for your protection. For example, an agent knows the law in California requires a carbon monoxide detector in the house. A seller may not know this. When the appraiser comes out, they will inform the seller who may not know anything about that. It is not so much about saving money, as it is about the disclosures and what you have to give a buyer when you sell your home. When you use a Realtor®, you are protected. Also, Realtors® have E&O insurance, which is another level of protection. When you work with a Realtor®, you should not have to worry about anything - all the necessary things that need to be done in a transaction get done, the correct way.

Communication

I believe buying a home is probably one of the scariest things one can do, especially when it is the first time you buy a home. The Realtor® needs to stay in constant communication and educate their client as to the process: what is going to happen, who is involved and why, who do they need to speak to for a given situation, etc. The Realtor® is always the center, the nucleus of this transaction, because we are dealing with the Lenders, Escrow, Inspectors, Buyers, and the Sellers. Everyone looks to us for direction as to the next step. If the Realtor® does not have good communication skills he will lose parts of the transaction, because he is not conveying the proper information so people can do their jobs.

Communication to the client goes back to education – you have to educate your clients. When the transaction is complete and the buyer gets his keys, they should almost feel like they can sell or buy a home themselves. When they can sit and explain to someone the exact processes of buying or selling a home, then you know you did a good job. That is the result of conveying and educating the buyer or seller, through communication.

You build a good and trusting relationship with a client simply by letting them know exactly what is happening. There is nothing worse than getting a phone call from an escrow officer or a lender, stating your client is upset because you are not communicating with them. To avoid this, you must stay in constant communication.

My Career

The focus of my career now is about being able to help others. I was the first one in my family to go to college. After I went, my sister, my brother, and now my nieces and nephews are going to college. Also, my nieces and nephews are now becoming homeowners in their early 20's!

Buying my first home was actually a fluke. After I became a Realtor®, I realized my real estate agent was actually a terrible agent. I had no idea what was happening, which goes back to why it is important to educate your clients. My landlord was a Realtor®, and she just showed up one day and said, "Get in the car." I was renting her four bedrooms, one bath house for $600 a month.

I got in her car and she drove a couple of blocks down the street and said, "See this house here? Do you like it?" I said, "Yes, it's okay." She said, "It is a little nicer than where you live now." And I agreed. She said, "Do you know that if you bought this house, your payment would actually be about $550 a month?" I said, "Okay..." And then she just looked at me and said, "Do you want to buy it?" I sat there thinking, "What on earth is going on here?"

The next thing I know, she had me sitting with a lender who ran my credit and said I qualified. My landlord proceeded to say, "Okay, sign here...sign here...sign here. As a matter of fact, I owe you back the deposit for the rent and I am not going to charge you this month's rent, so that'll be your deposit for your home." And I said, "Okay." And I signed, signed, and signed. About three weeks later, I got a phone call from the lender who said, "You need to come in and sign some documents." She did not even say they were loan documents - I know what they are now. That's how I came to own my first home. After I got my real estate license, I did some research and found out she sold me that house, and sold the seller another house she had listed. There were three houses in that chain. In order for one to close, she had to close the other, and so on. The reason she was so eager to get me into that home and not charge me deposits, was because she was making so much money off the transactions.

She was not looking out for my best interests. She wanted to close three transactions in a row. I had no idea what had happened, all I knew was I owned a home.

My roommates and I moved in, and then the entrepreneur side of me started coming out. I charged my roommates $200 each per room, plus a quarter of utilities. So my roommates technically paid all my mortgage payment, leaving me a little bit of extra money.

I eventually sold that home and made $110,000 profit. I bought another home, where my wife and I first lived and then sold that one and built the home we live in now. We have been here for eleven years. My oldest son is seven and my little one is five. I have a nineteen year old from a previous relationship. My wife and I have been together seventeen years - we had a lot of fun traveling and doing a lot of things before we had children.

In real estate, I very much enjoy building relationships. I enjoy my daily interactions with people, not just my clients, but also agents who I work with and agents who work for me. Communication skills are definitely a large part of my success because when I am dealing with people, I care about what they think and say. I remember their needs and goals and I keep them in the forefront of my mind when working with them.

I am a partner in a company called Miramar International. In the city of Bakersfield, we have over 250 agents who work with us. We have seven offices in Bakersfield, one office in Fresno, and we just opened an office in Glover Beach as we continue to expand. We are the largest real estate firm in Bakersfield and Kern County, with the largest volume of sales and agent count.

The success of my business goes back to relationships. The success of hiring agents is relationships. When I speak with agents, they really feel like I care about them, because I do. I want to know about their kids, their family, their parents, and how everyone is doing – because it all matters.

About the Author

Tony Ayon

Miramar International
Office: 661.322.7000
Mobile: 661.201.7618
Fax: 661.322.7012
tonyayon.miramar@gmail.com
www.bakersfieldareahomes.com

Tony was born into a large family in Mexicali, Mexico, with 8 brothers and sisters. Raised in Shafter, in an immigrant farm worker family, Tony quickly learned the value of work ethic. Through his humble beginnings, Tony understood the need for quality education. He achieved high marks in high school, and went to Cal State Bakersfield (1992-1996).

Tony's introduction to real estate came while working for Mercy Housing. There he quickly found his desire to obtain a real estate license, and eventually start his own company. He has been part owner of Coldwell Banker Delano (2004-2006), Universal Realty and Investment (2006-2008) and the first Keller Williams office in Bakersfield (2008-2011). In 2011, he partnered with Dan Shanyfelt, and together they established Miramar International, using a successful and innovative real estate model, attracting large numbers of quality agents in the area. His vision of an agent-centric real estate brokerage has grown to over 250 agents in 9 offices (one in Fresno and one in the Central Coast), and is the largest real estate brokerage in Bakersfield and Kern County.

As a real estate Broker, Tony has always valued keeping a strong relationship with all of his agents. He does so by being accessible, teaching, training, and advising his Realtor® associates regularly. His encouragement for continuing education is one of his biggest mantras. Tony also maintains a high production level of his own, in addition to his achievements as a Broker. He works with a large number of both sellers and buyers, and has always strived to maintain the utmost quality of service to all his clients. Tony serves the local real estate community through the Bakersfield Association of Realtors®, as member or chairman of various committees over the years, including Education, R-Gov, Partnership, Cultural Diversity, Golf Tournament, and is the current President of the Women's Council of Realtors®.

Along with his professional success, Tony is a dedicated family man, with three energetic sons. He is a reliable husband, father, uncle, brother, son, and grandson, and maintains a close relationship with his large extended family. He is also dedicated to community service and charitable causes. Tony founded his first non-profit organization at the age of 18, and he is the founder and current President of the Real Estate Professional Family Relief Fund. He is also actively involved in Mercy Housing, American Heart Association, Kern Probation Department Family Relief Fund, and Shafter Boxing Program.

Conclusion

As mentioned in the Introduction, we feel that the content provided by these carefully chosen Realtors® exceeded our expectations, and now that you've had a chance to read the book, we hope you feel the same way!

Whether you are already a homeowner and thinking of selling, or you are just starting out and looking forward to purchasing your first home, we hope that the information provided in this book has helped you.

The co-authors of this book are top-notch, well respected Realtors®. Their combined experience in the challenging field of real estate can be of great use to you when you are navigating thorugh the sale of your home or the purchase of a new home.

www.ingramcontent.com/pod-product-compliance
Lightning Source LLC
Chambersburg PA
CBHW051458170526
45166CB00001B/290